Between Good
and Ghetto

The Rutgers Series in Childhood Studies

The Rutgers Series in Childhood Studies is dedicated to increasing our understanding of children and childhoods, past and present, throughout the world. Children's voices and experiences are central. Authors come from a variety of fields, including anthropology, criminal justice, history, literature, psychology, religion, and sociology. The books in this series are intended for students, scholars, practitioners, and those who formulate policies that affect children's everyday lives and futures.

Edited by Myra Bluebond-Langner, Distinguished Professor of Anthropology, Rutgers University, Camden, and founding director of the Rutgers University Center for Children and Childhood Studies

Advisory Board

Between Good and Ghetto

African American Girls and Inner-City Violence

Nikki Jones

Rutgers University Press

New Brunswick, New Jersey, and London

LIBRARY OF CONGRESS CATALOGING-IN-PUBLICATION DATA

Jones, Nikki.
    Between good and ghetto : African American girls and inner city
violence / Nikki Jones.
        p.   cm.—(Rutgers series in childhood studies)
    Includes bibliographical references and index.
    ISBN 978–0–8135–4614–8 (hardcover : alk. paper)—ISBN
978–0–8135–4615–5 (pbk. : alk. paper)
    1. Inner cities—United States.   2. African American girls—
Social conditions.   3. Children and violence—United States.
I. Title.
    HT164.U6J66   2010
    305.23089'96073—dc22   2009000768

A British Cataloging-in-Publication record for this book is available
from the British Library.

Visit our Web site: http://rutgerspress.rutgers.edu

Manufactured in the United States of America

With gratitude for the stories shared and hope for the future

CONTENTS

PREFACE AND ACKNOWLEDGMENTS

I RETURNED TO PHILADELPHIA SEVERAL TIMES while completing this book. Some of the neighborhoods I once visited have undergone substantial changes: a block of row houses is replaced by new housing or a notorious high school is razed. Other blocks seem completely unchanged—a drive through these neighborhoods evokes the same feeling of isolation as it did when I began this project in 2001.

The picture on the cover of the book was taken during one of these return trips to the city. The vibrant mural covers the outside of a Black beauty salon in West Philadelphia. I returned to the shop several months after the picture was taken, when I was in the area to give a talk at Rutgers University's Center for Childhood Studies in Camden, New Jersey, across the river from Philadelphia. I was on a mission to locate the artist, identified only as "Marlin N" in the mural, and to request his permission to use a photograph of his work for the book's cover.

I took a cab to the hair salon the morning of my talk. The small, brightly colored beauty shop looks like many neighborhood hair salons in Black communities throughout the city. It has three chairs for cuts and styling, a hair drying section, and two shampoo chairs. A woman in her early twenties was shampooing the hair of a client when I arrived.

"Good morning," I said, "are you the owner?"

"What happened?" she asked with a level of concern that made me wonder if she thought I was a detective.

"Nothing happened," I reassured her.

I quickly explained that I was looking for the artist of the mural on the outside of her shop. She said that a few other people have also come by to ask about the artwork, which she commissioned when she opened the shop a couple of years ago. The artist is a young man in his twenties. He had only wanted something like ninety dollars for his work, she said, but she insisted on paying him more. I explained to her that I would like to use a photo of the mural for the cover of a book that I'm writing. She said that once she finished what she was doing she'd call around for Marlin's information. It looked like she was washing the perm out of a woman's hair and I was careful not to distract her for too long. The cream applied to the roots of your hair to straighten it can easily burn your scalp if left in your hair for even a moment too long. After giving her client a thorough rinse, she dried her hands and picked up her cell phone: "A lady here is looking for Marlin," I heard her say. She told the person on the other line that I wanted to use his artwork for a book. After a few moments, she hung up. The person on the other end of the line is going to give Marlin a call and he'll call us after he gets the message, she tells me.

As we waited, she asked me about my book: "What's it about?" I provided the shorthand answer that I've shared with many people over the last few years: African American girls and inner-city violence. This resonated with her immediately. She begins to tell me a story about her teenaged sisters, who are being harassed by a group of girls in the neighborhood. She wants to do the "right thing," in her words, and is working with school and juvenile justice officials to manage the situation. However, she also believes strongly that she has to be prepared to physically battle for her sisters when necessary. She and her mother have both had to fight for her sisters, she tells me. Her shop's windows have been broken and she was also physically injured during a retaliatory battle with these girls. She is concerned about further consequences to her economic livelihood.

A customer joins our conversation about girls' fights, sharing a story about a South Philadelphia girl who was hit in the face with a padlock, requiring over a hundred stitches to her face. I listen as they offer theories about what's happening with girls in the neighborhood. We share our concern about battles among girls that are now escalated with the use of social networking websites like MySpace and Facebook as we wait for Marlin's call. The shop owner also expresses a desire that is familiar to me after researching and writing this book: She wants to save up enough money to leave the neighborhood for good.

During a break in the conversation, I shared the title of the book with the shop owner and her customer: *Between Good and Ghetto: African American Girls and Inner-City Violence.*

"That's right," the shop owner responds as her customer nods affirmatively. They know the dilemma I describe in the following pages well. For this shop owner, the choice between doing what is right and what is necessary is not theoretical. She lives it each day.

After about twenty minutes, Marlin calls. We talk for a few moments and he gives me permission to use his artwork. I take down his contact information and promise to be back in touch soon. I thank the shop owner for connecting me with Marlin. I take a postcard with the store's address and promise to send a copy of the book after it is published. I tell the shop owner that I'll let her know when I return to the area. I leave the shop with a sense of gratitude and relief. I was drawn to Marlin's mural because it reflects the strength and sensitivity that is regularly revealed in inner-city girls' accounts of how they manage violence in their lives. The outward gaze of the woman in the mural reminds me of how many girls are focused on a better future for themselves. Much like this shop owner, they want to be somebody, oftentimes, somewhere else. The adolescent girls in this book are, like many inner-city residents, trying to live good lives while also accounting for the realities of life in distressed urban neighborhoods. As they do so, they encounter serious dilemmas with real-life consequences. This book offers an ethnographic account of how African American, adolescent girls reconcile these dilemmas and the gendered consequences of their doing so.

I am grateful to a large number of people for their support, encouragement, and advice over the last eight years. Professors Elijah Anderson, Robin Leidner, and Lawrence Sherman provided substantial support during the earliest drafts of this book. I am especially grateful to Elijah Anderson for his ongoing mentoring and guidance. Tukufu Zuberi, Camille Charles, and Demie Kurz also provided guidance and inspiration during my time at the University of Pennsylvania, as did a network of peers and friends. I am especially thankful for the friendship and conversations shared with Scott Brooks, Raymond Gunn, and Brooke Cunningham. This research also benefited from the support of the University of Pennsylvania Department of Sociology's Gertrude and Otto Pollak Grant for Summer Research (2003).

My promise of anonymity prevents me from thanking by name the team of doctors and counselors who worked at the city hospital from which respondents for this project were drawn. I am grateful for their invitation to work on this project. I extend my deepest appreciation to the project's transitional counseling team for their acceptance, engagement, and friendship over this time.

My colleagues in the Department of Sociology at the University of California, Santa Barbara, have provided an incredibly supportive and encouraging environment in which to complete this book project. France Winddance Twine provided extensive comments on the manuscript during the initial stages of revision. Sarah Fenstermaker's comments on my research and writing, along with her friendship, helped to improve the manuscript. Howard Winant continues to provide support for my research and writing and I am thankful for his enthusiasm, guidance, and friendship. I thank UCSB's Melvin Oliver, the SAGE Sara Miller McCune Dean of Social Sciences and Professor of Sociology, and Verta Taylor, chair of the Department of Sociology, for providing the resources necessary to complete this book. I am also grateful to Joe Castro and the Office of Academic Preparation and Equal Opportunity at the University of California, Santa Barbara, for providing generous support for manuscript preparation.

I thank Howard Becker and Robert Emerson for their helpful comments on early drafts of the manuscript. I also thank Joanne Belknap and the anonymous reviewers of the manuscript for their enthusiasm and recommendations. I am grateful to my editor, Adi Hovav, and the series editor, Myra Bluebond-Langner, for their encouragement and patience. The expert editing of Katherine Mooney, Heather Tirado Gilligan, and Barbara Glassman improved the manuscript greatly.

Finally, I am thankful for the love and encouragement of my parents, siblings, and in-laws, and the comic relief provided by my large brood of beautiful, smart, and funny nieces and nephews. I am forever indebted to my partner, Heather, whose contribution to the completion of this book is immeasurable.

*Between Good
and Ghetto*

Introduction

EARLY ON A WEEKDAY MORNING, a few min-
utes past the beginning of the school day, the line of students
that snakes into the front door of Martin Luther King High
School in South Philadelphia is no longer in sight.[1] Known
locally as "the prison on the hill," the large, grey building sits
atop a modest rise in one of the city's most troubled neighborhoods. Across the street from the school's main entrance is a
cement parking lot that sometimes doubles as a playground for
the neighboring public elementary school. The school is bor-
dered by a busy freeway on one side, and the Carver projects, a
collection of low-rise public housing apartments, on the other
side. Some units that once faced the school's back entrance
have been torn down. Slowly, they are being replaced by newly
designed structures that resemble small-scale town homes.

Police officers patrol the housing project's borders often,
and occasionally officers respond to calls from inside the high
school as well. On most days, however, uniformed guards
screen students and visitors and monitor school safety. Security
checks, endured by hundreds of Martin Luther King High's
students each morning, resemble the methodical screenings
required of all visitors to the city's courts, Criminal Justice
Center, and correctional facilities.[2] The high school's security
clearance procedures serve as a not-so-subtle reminder that for
many adolescent, inner-city boys and girls, the beginning of
the school day is not an escape from the threats of violence
that accompany life in the neighborhoods that surround the
school.

I approach the school's entrance and look on as a brown-skinned, teenaged girl a few steps ahead of me in line begins the screening process. She walks up the steps leading into the building, removes her backpack from her shoulder, and places it on a belt that moves the bag through an X-ray machine. Any metal object in her bag—a small knife or a razor blade, for example—should cause the machine to beep loudly. A moment passes—no beeps sound. As her bag moves through the X-ray machine, the student steps through a doorframe-shaped metal detector. Again, no beeps. A uniformed security officer stops her on the school side of the security gate. With little obvious prompting, she raises her arms parallel to the ground and looks to the side. I notice the seriousness of her expression as the security guard pats her down. He moves his hands under her arms and pats her back. He then quickly glides his hand across one outstretched arm and then the other. Then both hands travel down her sides. He moves both hands down her right leg and then her left. Finally, he squeezes her jeans pockets, lets out a short, nervous laugh, and releases her. She returns his laugh with a reluctant smile, grabs her bag from the security belt, and heads to the next table, just a few steps away. There she swipes her identification card in a card reader that is positioned in front of another guard, who is facing a monitor. The student's name and picture flash on the screen. The guard looks at the screen and then looks at her. She walks away. "Wait," the guard calls, "take your late pass." The student returns, takes her pass, and walks off in silence to begin her school day.

This girl's ritualized passage into her high school is just one indicator of how the circumstances of inner-city life, and especially the threat of interpersonal violence, structures teenaged girls' daily lives. Each school day morning, this adolescent girl, like her peers, receives the same screenings as the boys. Girls are not exempt from a hands-on search or from any other form of school-based surveillance simply because they are girls. Indeed, adolescent girls who attend troubled public high schools are increasingly subject to such screenings and sanctions as worries about school violence have expanded to include fights between girls. Such battles, including ones in which combatants brandish knives or box cutters, occur often enough to legitimate the fears of school administrators, teachers, parents, and students. The conversations I had over the three years of fieldwork for this book revealed the regularity of this violence. Teenaged girls described themselves or others getting "rolled on" or "jumped," or being involved in a "fair one" gone bad.[3] Like their male counterparts, girls could readily name someone who had been shot, robbed, or stabbed. Girls also disclosed witnessing this violence directly.

RACE, GENDER, AND
INNER-CITY VIOLENCE

Regular exposure to such dramatic violence is a consequence of coming of age in poor, Black neighborhoods in Philadelphia. A large, post-industrial, northeastern city, Philadelphia has experienced many of the same structural and economic changes that have impacted cities across the United States over the last thirty years, including deindustrialization, the concentration of poverty, and hypersegregation of its inner-city areas (Wilson 1980, 1987, 1996; Massey and Denton 1993; Anderson 1999).[4] In some respects, Philadelphia's central-city population has been hit harder by these changes than residents in comparable metropolitan areas. Philadelphia's poverty rate in 2000, the year before I began my field research, was 22.9 percent—almost double the national rate of 12.4 percent. Rates of concentrated poverty increased in Philadelphia during the 1990s as they leveled or declined in other metropolitan areas across the United States. In some South and West Philadelphia neighborhoods (where I conducted much of this study), between 30 and 40 percent of the resident population lives in poverty (Brookings Institution Center on Urban and Metropolitan Policy 2003, Pettit and Kingsley 2003).[5]

High rates of concentrated poverty are coupled with pronounced racial segregation in the city: the overwhelming majority of residents in the neighborhoods I visited are Black.[6] Philadelphia suffered from the seventh highest degree of segregation between Blacks and Whites in the country in 2000 (Brookings Institution Center on Urban and Metropolitan Policy 2003). In South and West Philadelphia, many blocks are dotted with large orange "condemned" signs, announcing that houses are being reclaimed by the city. These signs serve as visible markers of distress, as does the trash that accumulates in empty lots where abandoned homes once stood. There is often a visible police presence in poor, Black neighborhoods in the city, but many residents reject as naïve the idea that the police are there to protect them (Anderson 1999, ch. 2).[7] What parents and students often refer to as "out-of-control" neighborhood schools only add to the sense of strained resources and bleak prospects for the future of inner-city boys and girls. School counselors, who often insist that there are "good kids" in the schools, also occasionally use war analogies to describe their day-to-day attempts to counsel youth.

This combination of poverty and segregation tends to concentrate crime, violence, and other social ills in poor communities of color (Peterson and Krivo 2005; Wilson 1980, 1987, 1996; Massey and Denton 1993; Anderson 1999; Lauritsen and Sampson 1998; Sampson and Wilson 1995). Nationwide, violent crime rates have decreased dramatically since the mid-1990s, but in some large cities, including Philadelphia, homicide rates remain relatively high. In 2000 and 2001, the city recorded 319 and 309 murders, respectively. A dramatic spike in this number—to 380—in 2005 re-ignited local and national debates about inner-city violence (Philadelphia Police Department 2006; Anderson 2005; Zernike 2006).

Adolescent girls and boys, growing up in neighborhoods characterized by concentrated poverty and unpredictable violence, are necessarily preoccupied with survival (Anderson 1999). They understand that stray bullets do not discriminate between young and old, guilt and innocence, or boys and girls. Inner-city girls know that the settings of inner-city life, whether school buildings or row houses, neighborhood street corners or porch stoops, do not come with a special girls-only pass to live beyond the reach of violence. For these girls, as much as for the young men in their community, survival is a daily challenge. This book presents, in their own words and from their perspective, girls' descriptions of the violence that marks their world in various forms. Their accounts reveal the array of interpersonal and situational strategies they draw on as they navigate neighborhood and school settings where interpersonal violence is governed largely by a hypermasculine, eye-for-an-eye ethic.

This "code of the street," which Elijah Anderson has described as a system of accountability that governs "public social relations," especially interpersonal violence, rules distressed urban areas. This form of street justice takes hold where the presence of civil law is weak and thrives in social settings where formal institutions, like the schools or the police, have abdicated responsibility for protecting inner-city residents: "The code emerges where the influence of the police ends and personal responsibility for one's safety is felt to begin, resulting in a kind of 'people's law,' based on 'street justice'" (Anderson 1999, 10). A fundamental element of the code is the development of "a credible reputation for vengeance that works to deter aggression and disrespect, which are sources of great anxiety on the inner-city street" (10). A dialectical relationship between respect and manhood lies at the heart of the code: "For many inner-city youths, manhood and respect are two sides of the same coin" (91).[8] Poor, Black men and boys who live by the code enact a form of manhood that couples strength with physical dominance (Collins 2004, 210–212).[9] This complex relationship among masculinity, respect, strength, and dominance too often encourages poor, inner-city boys and men, and men in the underground economy in particular,[10] to resort to physical violence, or to risk their lives, in order to be recognized and respected by others *as men*.

The pressure to prove one's manhood was illustrated for me in a conversation with Craig, a young man who had deliberately checked his readiness to fight after being shot in the hip: "Yeah, I don't fight no more," he says, "I can't fight [because of injury]." He continues, "So, I really stop and think about stuff because it isn't even worth it . . . unless, I mean, you really want it [a fight] to happen . . . I'm going to turn the other cheek. But, I'm not going to be, like, wearing a skirt. That's the way you got to look at it." While Craig is prepared to check the need to fight, he also predicts that his newfound commitment to avoid fights will not stand up to the pressure of proving his manhood to a challenger. Craig is well aware of how another young man can use hard looks, verbal challenges, or slight bumps to communicate that he "really want [a fight] to happen." Once a challenger escalates a battle in this way, young men like Craig often feel as if they have few choices. He feels a great deal of pressure to demonstrate to his challenger, and his audience, that he isn't "wearing a skirt" or else be doomed to a series of confrontations and battles.

Adolescent girls who live in distressed inner-city neighborhoods have no manhood to defend. Yet, as the girls' accounts presented in this book reveal, they do have many reasons to be as preoccupied with protecting themselves from threats of violence. Through observation, instruction, and experience, inner-city girls, no less than boys, learn how reputation, respect, and retaliation—the fundamental elements of the code of the street— organize their social world (Anderson 1999, 63; Jones 2008).[11]

This shared understanding of the code was reflected during my interviews with adolescent girls and boys who were involved in violent incidents. Girls' accounts regularly revealed the common belief that you must be ready to demonstrate a willingness to fight as a way to deter ongoing challenges to one's well-being. "Sometimes you got to fight," Danielle, a recent high school graduate who grew up in the projects, explained to me, "[you got to] get into that type of battle to let them now that I'm not scared of you and you can't keep harassing me thinking that it's okay." Danielle's words echoed the beliefs of a young man I interviewed. Robert, an eleventh grader who is also a resident of a neighborhood where the code operates, told me, "Sometimes you do got to, you do got to fight. Cause you just got to tell them that you not scared of them."

Neither Danielle nor Robert had long fighting histories when I met them. They valued school and were hopeful about their futures. Yet, their comments, like those other adolescent girls and boys shared with me, revealed an appreciation of a shared system of accountability, "the code of the street," which encourages young people—teenaged girls and boys—to present a "tough front" and, depending on the situation, to fight, as a way to discourage future challenges to one's personal security in school and neighborhood settings.

BETWEEN GOOD AND GHETTO

The need to avoid or overcome dangers throughout their adolescence presents a uniquely gendered challenge for girls who grow up in distressed inner-city neighborhoods. As a system of accountability, gender reflects widely held beliefs, or normative expectations, about the "attitudes and activities appropriate for one's sex category." During interactions and encounters with others, children and adults evaluate themselves and others in light of these normative gender expectations in ways that reinforce or challenge beliefs about the natural qualities of boys and girls, and especially the essential differences between the two (West and Zimmerman 1987, 127; West and Fenstermaker 1995).[12] Generally, women and girls who are able to mirror normative expectations of femininity during their interactions with others—for example, by assuming a passive demeanor and presenting an appearance that does not significantly deviate from the standards of mainstream culture or local preferences—are evaluated by adults (e.g., family members, teachers, counselors) and by peers as appropriately feminine girls or *good* girls. Meanwhile, girls or women who seem to violate perceived gender boundaries by embracing stereotypically masculine behaviors (e.g., strength, independence, and an outwardly aggressive demeanor) often are disparagingly categorized as "unnaturally strong" (Collins 2004, 193–199).

The intersection of gender, race, and class further complicates the degree to which girls measure up to gender expectations. African American, inner-city girls in the United States are evaluated not only in light of mainstream gender expectations but also by the standards of Black respectability: the set of expectations governing how Black women and girls ought to behave. These are reflected in images of "the Black lady"—think Claire Huxtable from the popular 1980s sitcom *The Cosby Show*—the middle-class, Black woman who reflects many of the expectations of White, middle-class femininity (Collins 2004, 139–140; see also Higginbotham 1993, 204–205).[13] Black ladies distance themselves from behavioral displays of physical aggression or overt sexuality that are commonly associated with poor or working-class Black women. Black women and adolescent girls whose shade of skin color, body size, attitude, or demeanor deviate even slightly from mainstream expectations of femininity or Black female respectability are especially vulnerable to the formal and informal sanctions that accompany such gender violations (Cole and Guy-Sheftall 2003; Collins 2004; Richie 1996; Keith and Herring 1991).[14]

Inner-city girls who live in distressed urban neighborhoods face a gendered dilemma: they must learn how to effectively manage potential threats of interpersonal violence—in most cases this means that they must work the code as boys and men do—at the risk of violating mainstream and local expectations regarding appropriate feminine behavior. This is a uniquely difficult dilemma for girls, since the gendered expectations surrounding girls' and women's use or control of violence are especially constraining. Conventional wisdom suggests that girls and women, whether prompted by nature, socialization, or a combination of the two, generally avoid physically aggressive or violent behavior: girls are expected to use relational aggression and fight with words and tears, not fists or knives. Inner-city girls, like most American girls, feel pressure to be "good," "decent," and "respectable." Yet, like some inner-city boys, they may also feel pressure to "go for bad" (Katz 1988) or to establish a "tough front" (Anderson 1999; Dance 2002) in order to deter potential challengers on the street or in the school setting. They too may believe that "sometimes you do got to fight"—and sometimes they do. In doing so, these girls, and especially those girls who become deeply invested in crafting a public persona as a tough or violent girl, risk evaluation by peers, adults, and outsiders as "street" or "ghetto."

Among urban and suburban adolescents, "ghetto" is a popular slang term that is commonly used to categorize a person or behavior as ignorant, stupid, or otherwise morally deficient.[15] Inner-city residents use the term to describe the same kinds of actions and attitudes Elijah Anderson termed "street orientation." Analytically, the pairs "ghetto" and "good," or "street" and "decent," are used to represent "two poles of value orientation, two contrasting conceptual categories" that structure the moral order of inner-city life. In inner-city neighborhoods, the decent/street or good/ghetto distinctions are powerful. Community members use these distinctions as a basis for understanding, interpreting, and predicting their own and others' actions, attitudes, and behaviors, especially when it comes to interpersonal violence (Anderson 1999, 35). There is also a gendered dimension to these evaluative categories: good or decent girls are "young ladies" while "ghetto chicks" are adolescent girls whose "behaviors, dress, communication, and interaction styles" contrast with mainstream and Black middle-class expectations of appropriate and respectable femininity (Thompson and Keith 2004, 58).

The branding of adolescent girls as ghetto is self-perpetuating, alienating the institutional forces that protect good girls and forcing adolescent girls who work the code of the street to become increasingly independent. Girls who are evaluated by adults or peers as ghetto, as opposed to those evaluated as good, ultimately may have the code as their only protection in the too often violent inner-city world in which they live. Their efforts to protect themselves put them at risk of losing access to formal institutional settings like schools or the church, where girls who mirror normative gender expectations—girls who are perceived by others as good—can take some refuge. Yet, even for those good girls, this institutional protection is inadequate—they are aware that they may become targets in school or on the street and they too feel pressure to develop strategies that will help them successfully navigate their neighborhoods. Thus, inner-city girls find themselves caught in what amounts to a perpetual dilemma, forced by violent circumstances to choose between two options, neither of which offers the level of security that is generally taken for granted in areas outside of urban poverty.

Of course, real people—and perhaps especially adolescents—do not fit neatly into only one of two conceptual categories. My conversations with girls about their experiences with violence, along with my observations of their actions and conversations with others, revealed that girls astutely worked the code *between* the equal and opposing pressures of good and ghetto. From this social location, girls are able to challenge and manipulate the constraining social and cultural expectations embedded in gender and the code, depending on the situation. Elijah Anderson defines the activity of adapting one's behavior to the set of rules that govern a situation—decent or street, good or ghetto—as "code switching." Inner-city families and youth, most of whom strive for decency, put a "special premium" on the ability to "switch codes and play by the rules of the street," when necessary (1999, 36, 98–106). Of course, this act is complicated for girls whose working of the code is likely to challenge expectations regarding appropriate feminine behavior. Inner-city girls work the code with the understanding that they are always accountable to these gendered expectations and that gender violations are likely to open them up to a series of public or private sanctions. Girls' lives seemed to be defined by this everyday struggle to balance the need to protect themselves with the pressure to meet normative expectations associated with their gender, race, and class positions. Girls' accounts of how they manage these expectations, including how they work the code, defy any simple categorizations or stereotypical evaluations of girls as *either* good or ghetto. Instead, girls' accounts of violent incidents reveal that they embrace, challenge, reinforce, reflect, and contradict normative expectations of femininity and Black respectability *as* they work the code. Girls' accounts of navigating inner-city adolescence are characterized by this fluidity.

As I describe in the following pages, girls who are invested in being perceived by others as good tend to have a limited fighting history. They also typically have a network of family members who are committed to isolating (or at least buffering) them from actual and potential dangers of the street. Nevertheless, they understand how the code organizes social life in troubled neighborhoods. They may be reluctant to engage in physical battles, but they have also learned that "sometimes you got to fight." Even as they work the code, enacting displays of strength or aggression typically expected from boys, these adolescent girls (whom I describe in the following pages as "good girls") indicate an acceptance of fundamental elements of mainstream femininity and Black respectability. These expectations, in turn, modulate the way these girls handle conflict and violence in neighborhood settings. Their general commitment to presenting themselves in ways that conform to normative expectations is typically rewarded by adults. In the school setting, teachers and counselors are likely to treat girls who conform to gender expectations in ways that reaffirm their public personas as young ladies who are good and appropriately feminine. These girls' peers, and particularly their female peers, however, may observe such girls' appearance, attitude, and behavior—their "presentation of self" (Goffman 1959)—as evidence that these girls think they are better than their peers (i.e., that "they think they are all that"). For their part, these girls often conclude that other girls are "jealous." These competing perceptions often either instigate or are used to justify physical battles between girls. In other words, what protects and insulates them is at the same time their point of entry for violent conflict. This complexity is characteristic and illustrates how girls who may otherwise gravitate toward a set of behaviors or beliefs that are commonly perceived as appropriately feminine and essentially good get caught between good and ghetto.

In contrast to girls who see themselves as good girls, girls who see themselves as fighters tend to view life as an ongoing battle. They seem ready to fight at the slightest of provocation, even seeking out opportunities to prove their reputations by courting conflict or by engaging in the kinds of "campaigns for respect" (Anderson 1999, 68) that are common among inner-city boys. These girls are generally aware that others consider them outsiders, either because of their physical attributes or their behavior. Girls who are known for fighting and winning, whom I describe in the book as girl fighters, embrace those elements of the code that directly challenge gendered expectations associated with White, middle-class femininity and Black respectability. These girls may come to embrace this outsider status with confidence and without apology, often to the disappointment or frustration of those who would prefer that they look or act more like good girls. Yet, girl fighters may also be striving for decency in ways that are not obvious to most outsiders. Understanding how girls reconcile the gendered dilemmas that accompany working the code, whether they identify as good girls or fighters, expands and enriches our understanding of African American, inner-city girls' beliefs and behaviors, and deepens our understanding of how the contemporary circumstances of life in distressed inner-city neighborhoods shape their social world. In the chapters that follow, I offer a rich description of how inner-city girls use a range of resources and strategies, including aggressive or violent posturing or behavior, to actively and continuously make sense of and overcome the challenges that so frequently threaten their well-being, and the gendered consequences of these strategies.

Gaining Access: Girls in the VRP

I began systematically exploring the role of violence in the lives of inner-city girls after I was invited to work as an ethnographer for a city hospital–based violence reduction project (VRP). Each of the adolescent girls I discuss in this book had voluntarily enrolled in the project, which targeted Philadelphia youth aged twelve to twenty-four. All program participants were treated in the emergency department following an intentional violent incident, and all had been identified by VRP staff as either moderate or high risk for injury from similar incidents in the future.[16] As a consequence of patterns of racial segregation within the city, almost all VRP enrollees were African

American. Once enrolled in the VRP, a random selection of youth was assigned to receive intervention from a team of counselors who, over the course of several months, visited the young people in their homes, offered referrals, and provided mentoring with the aim of reducing the risk of subsequent violent injury.

A conversation with Tracey, a VRP project counselor, piqued my curiosity about girls' experiences with violence early on. Tracey, who is African American and was in her early twenties at the time, graduated from the same public city high school that some of the teenagers she now counseled attended. She lived in one of the neighborhoods included in the VRP's target area and could walk to some home visits. During our conversation, which took place in one of the hospital's conference rooms, I asked Tracey whether there were girls in the project. She said that there were. In fact, at that time, she said, her entire caseload was made up of girls. Most of the girls she counseled entered the emergency room with cuts or bruises from fights at school. I asked Tracey what the girls she worked with were fighting about.

"About being disrespected—that's about it," she replied.

"Being disrespected?"

"Yeah."

"So how's that look? What does that mean?" I asked.

"They're always saying, like, 'Nobody talks to me like that' and all. And I'm like, 'Yeah, but would you rather die over something somebody said?'"

"Do they see death as a real risk?" I asked her.

"No, no. They just see getting beat up and getting laughed at, that's all. And I try to tell them that life is too short to just do stupid stuff. You can't argue over dumb stuff. I don't expect you to go to school and not fight anymore because that would just be too unreal. I was like, 'But time will tell.' I don't know. I don't know. I don't know. Just crazy. I'm like, 'Okay, ya'll

were fighting because she said your sneakers were ugly—okay . . .
and [laughs] where does the argument start at?'"

"Do they answer you? Do they tell you where the argument starts?" I asked.

"Yeah, they were, like, 'She said my sneakers were ugly, and I said this, and then she said this, and next thing you know this girl said this and we just all started fighting.'"

Tracey's claim that young women were fighting "about being disrespected—that's about it" foreshadowed the significant role that public displays of disrespect play in girls' accounts of how fights begin. Such an understanding of girls' fights challenges the popular assumption that girls fight *only* over the attention of boys. Tracey's admission, "I don't expect you to go to school and not fight anymore because that would just be *too unreal*," also indicated a deep familiarity with the normative order of aggression in this setting. My conversation with Tracey encouraged me to focus my attention on uncovering the strategies that girls used to navigate inner-city settings where threats of interpersonal violence are encountered regularly, and the consequences of these strategies for girls in their everyday lives.

Looking back, my fieldwork, which included participant observation, direct observation, and formal and informal interviews with VRP participants, unfolded in three stages, over the period 2001 to 2003. Each stage logically built upon data collection and analysis undertaken during the previous stage(s).[17] During the first phase, which lasted nearly a year and a half, I accompanied Tracey and other VRP counselors as they made home visits to meet individually with program participants.[18] I also attended VRP events and interviewed members of the program's counseling staff—most of whom grew up in the city and were personally familiar with many of the neighborhoods in which the young people they counseled lived. In addition to observing these meetings and events, I also conducted formal and informal interviews with adolescent boys and girls enrolled in the VRP. In the second phase of the study, which lasted about a year, I visited program participants on my own and conducted interviews with twenty-four adolescents, including fifteen African American girls and nine boys.[19] I had met some of these participants during fieldwork conducted over the previous year, while I was meeting others for just the first time.

The third and final phase of the study lasted about a year and included observations and in-depth, open-ended interviews with three young women who were enrolled in the VRP: Terrie, a self-described "fighter," Danielle, a self-described "punk" (a non-"fighter"), and Amber, a young mother involved with a violent partner. I met each of them for the first time during the second phase of the study and then met with each of them several times throughout the final year. I visited Terrie and Danielle in their homes; my contact with Amber took me into a variety of settings, from a group home, to Planned Parenthood, to the city's Criminal Justice Center. I used the time I spent with Terrie, Danielle, and Amber to explore in greater depth some of the key concepts that had emerged during the previous phases of my data collection and analyses. These focused, in-depth interviews and observations helped me clarify the particular strategies adolescent girls used to negotiate conflict and violence.[20]

Over time, I became an "observant participant" of interactions in the spaces and places that were significant in the lives of the young people I met (Anderson 2001).[21] These spaces included trolley cars and buses, a neighborhood high school, the city's family and criminal courts, and various correctional facilities in the area, among others. I also intentionally engaged in extended conversations with grandmothers, mothers, sisters, brothers, cousins, and friends of the young people I visited and interviewed. I often recorded my observations and interactions in these settings in my field notes and used them to complement, supplement, test, and, at times, verify the information

I had collected during interviews or observations with VRP participants. This approach allowed me, during the first phase of the project, to develop a sound understanding of the physical, spatial, and symbolic context in which young people encountered various threats of violence; during the second and third phases, it helped me critically examine the strategies young people used to negotiate conflict and violence in their everyday lives and the various consequences of those strategies.

THE ORGANIZATION OF THIS BOOK

The lives of the inner-city girls and young women I profile in this book are deeply influenced by violence of various kinds. It is not uncommon for adolescent, inner-city girls to witness or directly encounter gun violence associated with drug dealers' disputes, threats of interpersonal violence, or sexual and dating violence. The everyday world that shapes their ideas and actions is not, however, likely to be familiar to many readers. Thus, each chapter includes detailed descriptions of people, settings, and representative social interactions. Each chapter's main theme is introduced and illustrated using excerpts from interviews or observations and brief narratives in the first half of the chapter. In the second half, an extended ethnographic narrative with a particular respondent provides a more detailed demonstration of the chapter's main theoretical argument.

In chapter 1, I introduce some key settings that shape the social world of today's inner-city girls and show that these settings—schools, neighborhoods, and "the corner"—are not free from violence. Mothers and grandmothers who are raising girls in this environment need to help them prepare for facing serious challenges and I describe some of the ways in which inner-city girls are socialized into survival. In the next two chapters, I illustrate the gendered dilemmas that emerge when girls work the code and describe the situated strategies that girls develop to manage threats of interpersonal violence. I begin, in chapter 2, by examining how girls with limited fighting histories reconcile the expectations associated with being seen as a good girl with the very different attitudes and behaviors needed to successfully deter potential threats of interpersonal violence. In doing so, I illuminate how intersections of color, class, and gender inform what it means to be a good girl in today's inner city.

In chapter 3, I take a closer look at the challenges and experiences of the girls who craft a "fighter" persona. Unlike good girls, who are generally reluctant to engage in physical battles, girls who see themselves as fighters manage threats of interpersonal violence—that is, they work the code—in ways that directly and often deliberately challenge both mainstream and local expectations regarding appropriate feminine behavior. I draw on girls' own accounts of violent incidents to explain how they become fighters and to identify some of the benefits and sanctions that girls accrue as a consequence of presenting a carefully crafted tough front to peers and outsiders. I briefly consider the future prospects for girls who see themselves as fighters throughout adolescence.

In chapter 4, I move from discussing how girls manage threats of interpersonal violence to a related topic that is often downplayed or overshadowed by discussions of poor, Black inner-city men and boys: the problem of dating and sexual violence against adolescent, inner-city girls.[22] The structural and cultural context of inner-city life, including the emotional stress associated with deeply entrenched poverty and the constant social pressure to obey the rules and meet the expectations of manhood embedded in the code of the street, often encourage the use of violence against women and girls. I show some of the unique ways in which these circumstances shape teenaged girls' understanding of and response to gendered violence in their everyday lives.

In the fifth and final chapter, I consider what the experiences of the girls discussed in this book reveal about contemporary conceptions of gender, strength, and survival among women and girls in poor, Black communities. Historically, the material circumstances of poor women's lives in general, and those of poor Black women in particular, have required a commitment to raising girls to become strong women. Whether they understand themselves as good girls or chiefly as fighters, the adolescent girls I came to know embraced locally held beliefs about the value of female strength. This positive embrace and unapologetic expression of female strength, which contrasts with traditional White, middle-class conceptions of femininity, and the gendered expectations embedded in Black respectability, was considered necessary for Black women's survival and for the survival of the Black community. The adolescent girls profiled in this book showed themselves to be no less concerned with survival than were strong Black women and girls in earlier periods. However, in today's inner city, where the culture of the code organizes much of social life, what a girl has got to do to survive has taken on new meanings. In concluding the book, I address some of the far-reaching implications of these changes. I offer as well a brief consideration of the academic, programmatic, and policy responses that are necessary in order to make survival less of a struggle for future generations of African American inner-city girls.

CHAPTER 1

The Social World of
Inner-City Girls

MAINSTREAM AMERICAN SOCIETY commonly assumes that women and girls do not fight like boys and men. We like to think that women and girls shy away from conflict and physical aggression. Popular representations of mean girls who fight only with body language and relationships and not with fists or knives typify and reinforce mainstream beliefs about gender-based differences in the use of physical force (Simmons 2002; Wiseman 2003). Yet, not all girls can so easily cast aside any consideration of the use of physical aggression. Some girls, like those featured in this book, learn early on that they must be prepared to fight for their survival. Social scientists often overlook the fact that today's inner-city girl comes of age in the same distressed neighborhoods as those of her male counterparts. Inner-city girls are not isolated from the social consequences of racial segregation, concentrated poverty, and inner-city violence. As the narratives of the adolescent girls in this book show, inner-city girls are touched—figuratively, literally, and daily—by violence. In contrast to the relatively sheltered lives of middle-class, suburban girls, African American inner-city girls' lives are shaped by the salience of the drug trade, a widespread distrust of social institutions and social relationships, and regular exposure to chaotic and too often violent conditions, whether at school or in the neighborhood. These girls see other adolescent girls fight with fists and knives and sometimes they do so too.

The ethnographic observations, scenes, and portraits in this book show how the circumstances of inner-city life shape the social world of today's inner-city girl. These stories elucidate the settings that adolescent inner-city girls share with teenaged boys and men, yet show how gender mediates their interactions within the same social space. As with poor Black boys, the circumstances under which these girls live demand an understanding of how to manage threats of interpersonal violence in these settings. At the same time, socializing girls for inner-city survival presents new challenges and dilemmas for African American grandmothers, mothers, and "othermothers" who are bringing girls up in this setting.[1] These challenges, among others, are revealed in the ethnographic portrait of one inner-city girl's attempt to respond to a violent attack that concludes this chapter. Taken together, these stories highlight important aspects of the social world of inner-city girls and help us to better understand how those who care for these girls manage the chaos that too often characterizes their lives.

THE URBAN TERRAIN: SCHOOL,
THE BLOCK, AND THE CORNER

Like that of other adolescent girls in America, the social world of the inner-city girl is significantly shaped by her interactions and experiences in a few key settings, most notably, her home, her school, and her neighborhood. In some ways, urban public high schools are a lot like other large public high schools in urban and suburban areas around the country. The school days in urban high schools go through periods of relative calm and relative chaos. Between classes, students crowd the hallways in boisterous swarms. The schools' corridors and stairwells pulse with the high energy of adolescence. The noise fades as the hallways empty and the classrooms fill, echoing the daily rhythm of school life across the nation. But a lack of order, a sense that things are "out of control," as Naima, one my respondents, says, distinguishes many urban public schools from schools with more institutional support and economic resources.

During a visit to Martin Luther King (MLK) High, for example, I breathed in the lingering scent of marijuana that clings to some students as they make their way through the front-entrance security checks. Graduates and others familiar with the school suggested to me that security guards ignore students who arrive at school high on marijuana because the drug makes the young people less difficult to deal with. But even security violations the guards are actively interested in preventing—including bringing weapons onto school grounds— occur with regularity. Innovative students find ways around the security checkpoint; others are adept at fooling the school security systems. During the several-month period that I visited the "Prison on the Hill," for example, a group of teenaged girls entered the high school and, armed with box cutters, launched a violent lunchroom battle that drew much attention from the local news media. Inner-city residents feel that the violence in these schools is getting worse, especially among the girls. MLK High graduate Naima tells me that while the school was violent when she was a student, "it was more controlled better."

In many cases, Naima explains, conflicts at school are extensions of battles for respect both within and between neighborhoods: "It's just, like, a neighborhood thing. It, that's how it was when I was there, neighborhoods against neighborhoods." In Philadelphia, street numbers, one's block, or housing project affiliation are often used to distinguish cliques or sets within geographical regions of the city (for example, within North or South Philadelphia). Naima describes for me how territory is negotiated between neighborhoods: "Like out Carver [projects], that's where Martin Luther King High [is], and nobody from Twenty-third Street can come over there, but they go to school there. But they [Carver projects students] didn't like them [23rd

Street students], so it was a big thing." The way that students are assigned to high schools does not necessarily reflect these various affiliations, and brings together groups of teenaged girls and boys who are at times antagonistic towards each other for reasons that are rooted in these block-by-block distinctions.

While fights among adolescents are not unusual, anxiety around fights in inner-city schools reflects deep fears about lethal violence. In recent years, the use of weapons, especially guns and knives, has made school fights more dangerous. Naima comments on this difference:

"Like now, when I hear recent stories about MLK High School, like, they was shooting in one classroom and then they was starting fires. Like, none of that never happened when I was there. Like we had—what you call them?—metal detectors [and] like somebody got caught with some mace or something, but no guns or knives or none of that." Naima has heard that the high school is slated for closure. She, like many others in the neighborhood, finds not regret but relief in that possibility.

For urban adolescents who are coming of age in neighborhoods marked by a deeply entrenched drug trade, and the violence that commonly accompanies such activity, their observations, experiences, and interactions inside and outside of the school setting deeply inform their beliefs about safety, justice, and survival. For example, in recent years, "the corner," as it is described by youth, has emerged as a distinct social setting in the lives of inner-city adolescents. The corners of city blocks traditionally have served as hubs of local activity. These spaces have been well documented as anchors of social interaction and sites of social organization (Whyte 1943; Liebow 1967; Anderson 1978). In today's inner-city neighborhoods, the corner marks a geographic space of belonging for some and uncertainty for others. The corner, which is frequently the eye of the storm for much of the lethal violence that occurs in the neighborhood, is often marked, physically and symbolically, by groups of young Black men wearing baggy denim jeans and white T-shirts, or some other version of urban attire. Neighborhood residents typically know which corners are owned by the drug dealers, even though they may not know the names of the young men who crowd around the stoop nearest to the corner or hang out near the entrance to the local corner store. Indeed, residents are well aware that buying and selling illegal drugs are now primary uses of the corner space.

The corner is also a gathering place and a staging area (Anderson 1999) for some of the neighborhood's young men, and at times, young women, too. The corner is a prime location for social observation. Sometimes, young men sit or stand quietly, simply staring as people pass by; other times, the corner is noisy with the sounds of playful, flirtatious exchanges as young men and women casually evaluate one another. Young men may use the corner to prove something to their male peers; they may, for example, stake their claim to being somebody by deliberately, and without invitation, breaching the space of young women who pass by (Anderson 1978; Duneier 1999).

The adolescent boys and young men who sell drugs on the corner occupy several social status positions within the neighborhood. Their involvement in the illegal drug trade does not necessarily exclude them altogether from enacting their roles as brothers, sons, or boyfriends. At times, they may try to mimic some of the practices of the "old heads," older African American men who helped shape previous generations of children and young adults. They may look out for some residents and adopt a protective attitude toward others on the block, including those individuals they think may have a chance for finding success in the future in some legitimate activity.

Lauren, for example, a fourteen-year-old girl who shares a home in West Philadelphia with her mother, two older sisters, an older brother, and a niece, has been "adopted," in her words, by a former boyfriend of one of her sisters who regularly

spends time on the corner. Adult supervision is largely absent
from Lauren's daily life. Her grandfather—people dubbed her
his shadow—recently died; her mother works full time as an
office assistant. This is not to say that she is unloved: her mother
tries to maintain discipline and structure through weekly family
meetings, and threatens to send her to live with her father, who
has relocated to Florida, when she acts up.

Like many others in the neighborhood, Lauren is familiar
with the boys on the corner: she knows that they sell drugs
there. She also knows that the corner is where her old head
works. I ask Lauren about the role of the old heads. "They be
acting like they your older brother, looking out for you," she
explains. The young men on the corner use their location to
keep an eye on the activities of neighborhood residents, including adolescent girls like Lauren. Her old head encourages her to
stay out of trouble, she says, and he knows when she should be
in school. Lauren provides an example of how her self-styled
street mentor monitors her behavior. After she left school early
one day and walked by the corner on her way home, "he got all
up on me like, 'Why ain't you at school?' I was like, 'Dag, you
know you ain't my dad.'"

But the perceived positive contributions individual young
men involved in the local drug market may make to their
neighborhoods are offset by the street violence that accompanies the drug trade. As a result, relationships between the young
Black men and boys who hang out on the corners and neighborhood residents are tenuous. Some adolescent girls may relate
to certain of the men on the corner as big brothers or as father-
like figures. Other neighborhood residents may even express
their frustration with a social structure that has limited young
men's ability to envision opportunities for making a living outside of the drug trade. Still others, particularly older urban residents, are likely to express dismay over the corner crowd.
"They could be anything they want," one grandmother tells

me, the disappointment evident in her voice. "They don't have to be out there selling drugs."

MAKING SENSE OF DEATH: "HE DIDN'T DO ANYTHING"

The salience of drug markets in inner-city neighborhoods has not been diminished by the never-ending war on drugs, which has locked some families into generational cycles of poverty and official criminality. In the most economically compromised areas of Philadelphia, some young Black women who sell drugs make themselves vulnerable to the same types of violence that threatens the lives of their male counterparts.[2] In addition, and perhaps more commonly, young women hold drugs for young men who are selling in school or in the neighborhood. Syreeta, who grew up in the notorious Carver projects and now attends a predominantly White, elite liberal arts college in the Northeast, confided that she had made "a little money" during her middle-school years by assisting a classmate who sold drugs during the school day: "My job in helping him was just holding his money." Even holding money is dangerous because of the unexpected and oftentimes horrific nature of drug-related violence. Many of the young people I spoke with quickly recalled friends, relatives, or neighbors who had been caught in drug-related violence. A common thread of these remembrances is how this violence dramatically interrupts the life chances of otherwise innocent young people.

Syreeta witnessed a nightmarish episode of violence while visiting her half-sister's father in North Philadelphia. Despite the violence of her own area, she was unprepared for the shock: "I remember one time it was me and my cousin" she recalls, "and a couple of our friends, and we're walking down Twenty-ninth Street, just walking on one summer day." Walking ahead of them was a young boy named Shawn, whom most neighborhood residents knew as "a good kid," she says. Unlike other young men his age who spent time on the streets and the corner, "[Shawn] stayed in the house," Syreeta remembers, "like, a lot." He had a simple weekday routine that, she says, most residents on his block were familiar with: "He would come home from school and be in the house." During school breaks, his mother worked to insulate Shawn from the potential dangers of the street by filling his day with activities; Syreeta remembers, "In the summertime, his mom would have him in summer camps."

Shawn's mother's efforts to insulate him from known and imagined threats ultimately failed. Syreeta explains: "We were both walking down the street and he's in front of the Jehovah's Witnesses' Kingdom Hall. He was standing in front of there talking to somebody he knew. We're like a half a block away, and some other guy was standing on the corner. So this car rolls around and start shooting." Syreeta and her cousins had learned at an early age what to do as soon as shots begin to ring out. "We all hit the ground," she says, but Shawn hesitated. "He was a little bit slow hitting the ground," Syreeta recalls, "and he got shot, and so did the guy who was standing like, five or ten feet away from him." Shawn later died from his gunshot wound. For Syreeta, the impact of witnessing such a violent scene endures today. "Like that really sticks out in my mind because it was an incident where—I think I may have been in like fourth grade at the time—and it was like, I distinctly remember being like, 'He didn't do anything.' Like, he was told to go to the store and come back and he was on his way to the store. He just stopped to talk to somebody and then, got caught."

In neighborhoods like the ones in which Shawn, Lauren, and Syreeta live, such tragic scenes are not extraordinary. Simmering tensions erupt in drug-related murders or over seemingly trivial slights or demonstrations of disrespect, such as hard stares or bumps, which, given the easy access to guns in distressed urban areas, can quickly escalate to serious or lethal violence. Such violent eruptions and the reactions to these incidents by the community and especially the police fuel fears about safety and survival in the inner city. These dramatic events—from crack house killings to deaths from stray bullets—deeply influence the social worlds of adolescent boys *and* girls growing up in the inner city. Among young people, including girls, these experiences shape perceptions of the necessity, utility, and consequences of aggression and violence.

SOCIALIZING INNER-CITY
GIRLS FOR SURVIVAL

Today's adolescent inner-city girl is no stranger to chaos, conflict, or violence—by the time she has reached her early teens she is aware that fights with fists, knives, and box cutters occur among girls in school and in her neighborhood. She knows that boys and men involved in the drug game are gunned down while plying their trade on street corners or city blocks and young, innocent bystanders sometimes die in the crossfire. It is difficult for inner-city girls and the women who care for them to embrace or express hope that the circumstances of inner-city life will ever change. In addition to raising girls to withstand the racism and sexism they are likely to encounter as grown-up Black women in America, mothers, grandmothers caring for their children's children, and othermothers, mired in the trenches of poverty, must now also teach girls how to manage the physical threats that they are likely to encounter in everyday life.[3] Socializing girls for this sort of survival—teaching them to figuratively and literally fight to protect their personal boundaries, for example—presents a dilemma for women who are trying to be good mothers and for those women who are committed to raising African American, inner-city girls to become respectable Black ladies. This is a dilemma that few middle-class mothers in suburban areas encounter.

It may be difficult for people who live in safe and stable neighborhoods to understand why some mothers may feel compelled to teach their daughters to become able fighters. Passing on such lessons to adolescent girls violates widely held beliefs about appropriate behavior for girls and seems far apart from commonly held understandings about what it means to be a good mother. My conversations with mothers and daughters who embraced these lessons revealed that mothers who encourage their daughters to become able fighters often believe that they are passing on a lesson that is necessary for a girl's survival in troubled neighborhoods. Oftentimes, mothers are instructing their daughters based on their own experiences as children in the same or similar neighborhood settings, when they too had to fight to protect themselves. Ms. Jackson, the mother of Neka, a teenaged girl with a tough demeanor, explained to me how she learned to fight in high school and felt compelled to pass this lesson on to her daughter. Ms. Jackson recalled one Christmas during her high school years when she received a down coat, then the height of style and an expensive gift. When she returned to school after Christmas break, some girls in her high school beat her up and tore her brand new coat. When she got home, her mother beat her as well for returning with a ripped coat.

After this incident, Ms. Jackson's then boyfriend taught her how to fight so she would not continue to get beat up by either the girls in her school or her mother. As a mother, Ms. Jackson also began to pass these lessons along, once it became clear to her that her children needed to know how to fight to survive in their neighborhood, where kids physically challenged other kids every day. This became particularly clear to her after Neka was seriously injured when a young boy kicked her in the stomach and into the inside of a trash can. Ms. Jackson recalls that Neka could not eat for two days after the incident. Once Neka recovered, Ms. Jackson repeated the instruction she received from her old boyfriend. After sharing this story with me, Ms. Jackson paused, and clarified that she was simply trying to be a good mom. Already, she had lost one son to the streets. She did not want her daughter to become a "statistic," she said. For mothers like Ms. Jackson, teaching their children—boys and girls—to physically defend themselves when they are not there to protect them is a key survival lesson that they feel responsible for passing along.

In addition to encouraging their daughters to become able fighters, some mothers I spoke to actively involved themselves in the interpersonal conflicts of their children. They may orchestrate a fight among adolescents or get their daughter's back in a fight, difficult as this may be for some readers to imagine. Generally, we expect parents to model behavior that discourages the use of violence. Yet, parenting styles also reflect a personal set of resources and experiences—emotional, psychological, economic, and social. These resources are not spread out equally among mothers or caretakers, and parents who live in distressed urban areas must account for potential threats of violence that are unique to inner-city life. Given the set of circumstances inner-city adolescents must face, it is not uncommon to encounter mothers who teach their daughters *not* to shy away from potential conflicts. Mothers who are more adept at negotiating complicated emotional situations and who want to model decent behavior for their children may encourage their daughters to avoid or ignore instigators, or to de-escalate a situation by talking it out. Yet, these mothers are also aware that such efforts may be wasted on other girls who have a point to prove about their own toughness. If these efforts fail, these same girls may be encouraged to fight as a final resort: "If you didn't [fight] you got picked on more," one mother explained to me.

When ongoing animosities between adolescent girls escalate to the level of physical conflict, mothers may also be called on to come to the scene of a fight to take on a supervisory role.

As Danielle explained, her mother came to one conflict not to stop the fight her daughter seemed likely to be caught up in, but to make sure it did not turn into what she described as a "bloodbath" (see chapter 2). The fight where DeLisha, a teenaged girl, was cut on the arm (see chapter 3) was also arranged by a mother, showing that a supervisor cannot always safeguard against serious escalations of fistfights. The conflict began, DeLisha explained, when she "had words" with a neighborhood girl and a fight erupted. When it ended, a second battle began: "Once the fight was over, my girlfriend, Teka, said that she wanted to fight her [the neighborhood girl]. So, I wasn't going to leave her around there [by herself]. So, I stayed around there, and her mom said, 'She doesn't want to fight Teka, she wants to fight DeLisha again.' So, me and her were about to fight." Encouraged by her mother, the neighborhood girl once again took DeLisha on. Perhaps overwhelmed by the pressure to meet her mother's demands, this adolescent girl violated the grounds of a fair fight. Using a box cutter secured a definitive victory, one that was sure to end the conflict between the two teenagers, at least in the short term.

Mothers with credible street reputations as tough women may also abandon their customary supervisory role and insert themselves into conflicts, and adolescent girls whose mothers have a fighter's reputation can also trade on their parent's strength. Peers may avoid conflicts with her for fear that confrontations might escalate into a physical fight between mothers. Syreeta, for example, knows that her mother's reputation shielded her from many fistfights with girls when she was growing up in the projects. They knew, she explained, that if "you get into a fight with me, then my mom is going to yell at your mom and my mom might fight your mom."

For much of the twentieth century, the major threat to a poor, Black girl's well-being was considered to be the racism and sexism that would be directed at her by the outer, Whiter world.

Stories of Black mothers raising their daughters to overcome the multiple obstacles they are likely to encounter reflect the special attention African American mothers give to teaching their daughters how to survive such oppressive conditions. These survival lessons, however, have not typically included an embrace of a *physical* strength that can be *directed at other Black girls*. This lesson has only emerged as necessary over the last few decades as inner-city life itself has gotten harsher and the consequences for failing to adequately protect oneself have grown more dire. Today, inner-city, adolescent girls and their mothers are aware that their home front has turned into its own battleground. In this urban battlefield, girls and their mothers learn that skin color does not guarantee solidarity, and Black life, even innocent Black life, is expendable: Black youth fight, injure, and kill other Black youth.[4]

This awareness of the circumstances of inner-city life influences how mothers socialize the girls under their care. Black mothers raising daughters in today's inner city continue to work to instill a strong sense of independence in their daughters and encourage them to recognize their own essential role in maintaining their own well-being. They teach young women to identify and respond to actual and potential threats, and encourage girls to realize that one of their most valuable resources is their own strength. By the time urban, adolescent girls reach their late teens they have internalized these lessons of self-reliance and independence, usually in a way that includes an acknowledgement that violence is a fact of inner-city life. Teenaged girls who have lived through especially challenging life circumstances may come to think of themselves as "grown." In everyday conversations, "grown" is a term used to describe adolescent girls whose level of maturity appears to be greater than what is typical for their chronological age. This mismatch between age and maturity is also likely to occur among girls who have come to terms with parental neglect or abandonment.

Other experiences that may contribute to a girl's accelerated sense of maturity include an early pregnancy, a level of financial independence (sometimes secured with an illegal hustle), or a history of taking care of herself or supporting others. Witnessing extreme expressions of violence, like the shootouts that sometimes accompany local drug dealing, also lead young women to consider themselves grown.[5] The combination of this appreciation for independence and accelerated maturity may make it difficult for mothers and grandmothers to communicate with their daughters or granddaughters effectively. In extreme circumstances, women may become frustrated and exhausted by their failed attempts to manage their daughters or granddaughters and may relinquish responsibility to school administrators, teachers, or even the juvenile or criminal justice system.

THE ROLE OF GRANDMOTHERS

Historically, Black grandmothers either have assisted in the care of children or have taken over care altogether (Collins 2000; Anderson 1994, 1999; Stack 1974; Gutman 1976). This remained true during the periods of violence that characterized much of inner-city life in the late 1980s and early 1990s, when women took in their grandchildren after their own children became casualties of the street, and this pattern continues today (Anderson 1999; Hunter 1997). The contemporary circumstances of inner-city life present physical, emotional, and financial challenges for grandmothers who are caring for their grandchildren. Wise grandmothers encourage their granddaughters to be good girls and to isolate themselves socially as a way to avoid violent interactions (see chapter 2). Grandmothers are also likely to emphasize the importance of formal education. In addition to encouraging young women to stay inside and study, grandmothers—especially when their children have histories of drug use, violence, or crime—frequently warn adolescent girls to avoid the dangers of the street, pointing out the areas of the neighborhood and the people they ought to avoid, especially the places and spaces where drug dealers work or hang out.

The knowledge and fear of such areas influences even the most mundane, everyday decisions. For example, during the preparations for a family party at a home in West Philadelphia, I listened as a grandmother instructed family members (including her children, grandchildren, and great-grandchildren) on where to buy a mixed salad for the party. When one of the adult daughters, who appeared to be in her early forties, announced, "I'm going to go to Green's," her mother cut in firmly, advising, "I wouldn't go there, that's a drug haven." As the assembled group gave the grandmother their full attention, she explained how the drug dealers hang out in groups in the area outside the entrance to Green's market. After a moment of silence during which the listening women pondered the grandmother's warning, the daughter responded, "They're all drug havens around this way!" and the others, amid laughter, confirmed, "I know that's right." In the end, the mixed salad was purchased at a store located outside of the neighborhood.

For teenaged girls, repeated warnings and attempts to constrain their social mobility may or may not have the desired effect. Some seriously heed the warnings and work to become the good kids their grandmothers want them to be. Others, however, find the approach taken by grandmothers too restrictive. Either way, grandmothers cannot insulate their grandchildren from involvement in all forms of interpersonal conflict, and in acknowledgement of this fact of inner-city life, some grandmothers also teach their granddaughters how to negotiate physical conflicts. When an adolescent girl gets into a fight and comes home crying, it is not altogether uncommon for a grandmother who realizes the importance of avoiding a reputation as a weak person to send her granddaughter back out for a "fair" fight. Grandmothers who encourage their granddaughters to meet battles head-on understand that in the inner city, you need not have a reputation as crazy or violent, but you must be able to fight your own battles when necessary or become vulnerable to future challenges. DeLisha's grandmother, for example, tried to teach her granddaughter how to protect herself. In explaining why she would not limit her own mobility in order to avoid the very real possibility of a second violent encounter with a girl who had wounded her with a box cutter, DeLisha asserted, "My grandma never raised me to look over my shoulder."

The orchestrations and interventions of mothers, along with the strict directives of grandmothers, encourage inner-city girls in their late teens to realize that they must be responsible for their own well-being, even those who have a network of friends or family that will get their back. Girls come to believe that they cannot naïvely expect anyone else to act on their behalf. Like many other inner-city residents, girls come to see many people as out for themselves and acknowledge that they too must not expect anyone else to make them safe. Ultimately, teaching adolescent girls how to physically defend their personal boundaries provides them with a resource that they need to navigate their neighborhood streets. At the same time, this kind of instruction also transmits an early and important lesson from one generation of Black women to the next: you are responsible for your own well-being. Such a lesson contrasts sharply with the socialization experiences of many middle-class, suburban youth.

In inner-city settings that are governed by the code of the street, women's attempts to socialize their children for survival often require that they adopt beliefs and behaviors directly opposed to mainstream expectations of appropriate femininity and the gendered expectations reflected in the image of the Black lady. What outsiders often have difficulty understanding, however, is that oftentimes, these actions and behaviors emerge from attempts to navigate extremely challenging and potentially life-threatening circumstances. Inner-city mothers, grandmothers, and othermothers must make "hard choices" about how best to socialize Black girls for survival. For many poor, African American women, and especially for those living in violent neighborhoods, the pressure to "regularly feel required to make hard choices among, at times, very poor options" is often the most stable condition of their lives (Richie 1996, 2). In this setting, it would be a great disservice for mothers or grandmothers *not* to teach the girls under their care how to protect themselves from potential threats of violence in the neighborhood. Still, it is a lesson that comes with complicated consequences: girls who embrace these lessons about strength and survival too deeply, for example, girls who fight all the time, risk confirming the most base stereotypes others hold about poor, Black women and girls.

The following narrative highlights the dilemmas faced by inner-city mothers and girls, and the hard choices made by one girl's mother who, like many poor, Black mothers, struggles with the choice to do what is right morally versus what is necessary. Shante's story also illustrates how one adolescent inner-city girl comes to learn that she must take an active role in defending herself from potential attacks. In practice, this realization means that girls like Shante must find a way to resolve conflicts without the help of formal institutions, such as the police.

SHANTE'S STORY

Shante, a sixteen-year-old African American girl, lives in South Philadelphia, near the Carver projects. She spends the majority of her time in the house, while her slightly older sister spends most of her time on the street. Shante, well aware of the potential dangers facing girls who spend much time on the street, worries about her sister. After a year of suspensions, punishments, and running away, Shante's sister was eventually "put away" in a residential detention center for young women. Her sister is "doing alright now," though. She has been assigned to a rehabilitation center and recently earned a home pass that allows her to visit for the weekend. Shante's younger brother has a chronic illness, but "he still go out there and have his fun like a normal teenager would," she says. Sometimes her brother runs into more than just fun outside. With his slight build, he is a frequent target of other young boys' public challenges: "He just got jumped recently."

Weekdays begin early for Shante. She transferred from Martin Luther King High School to Southwestern High recently, and must get up at six each morning in order to make it to school on time. After school, she usually returns home, where she watches television or talks on the phone. She socializes with a very small network of friends and family. A number of the teenaged girls in her social circle are already mothers, but Shante has no intentions of joining their club: "One of my friends got a baby. My old friend got a baby. My other friend got a daughter. All these friends got a lot of kids. That don't make no sense. It don't." Shante tells me that when she grows up, she would like to be "someone who delivers babies." Right now, she would be happy with a job in retail or even a position at a fast-food restaurant.

Shante has lived close to the Carver housing projects most of her life. She has been involved in the occasional fight, yet she has never considered herself a fighter. (See chapter 3 for a discussion of the distinction girls make between fighting occasionally and being a fighter.) When she was fifteen, another teenaged girl from the neighborhood bashed her in the head with a brick. Initially, Shante had no idea what had instigated this attack. In the months following the incident, she realized that it was a case of the "he say/she say," a common cause of fights between adolescent girls in this setting. The "he say/she say" begins when one person hears that another has said something derogatory about them. The original source of the rumor is not always

known. Shante explains, "I don't know who was going back
around saying this stuff [to the young woman who hit her] that
like, 'Yeah, Shante said she don't like the way you walk because
you bowlegged.'" What is alleged to have been said in a "he
say/she say" exchange is, as Shante recognizes, often far from
the truth: "How I'm going to judge someone I don't even know
them?" Shante asks. "How am I not going to like this girl just
because of the way she walk?"

In adolescent inner-city worlds, the he say/she say, even
when based on false rumors, can quickly escalate into physical
conflicts. Both parties' reputations in the neighborhood are
potentially at stake. One or both of the young women may
feel she has to respond to the he say/she say, either verbally or
physically.[6] Shante describes how the he say/she say interaction
unfolded in her case:

> After school, I left like ten minutes early [and] I seen her on
> the corner with . . . her boyfriend. And me and my friend
> walked to the store. . . . I walked her to the store, and she
> live in Carver projects and I live on Carver Street, so I said,
> "I'm going to walk you to the store," and I'm going to
> walk up Carver Street 'cause she was going that way any-
> way. So I'm walking, [my friend] goes to the projects 'cause
> that's where she live. I'm still walking straight [on Carver
> Street]. I was on my way home . . . I was just about to walk
> in the middle of the street [when] she grabbed me by the
> back of my hair and was hitting me with it [the brick]. I
> went to the hospital 'cause I had to get staples in my head
> and something was wrong with my wrist.

It is not uncommon for inner-city, adolescent girls who are
involved in serious physical conflicts to call on their mothers for
help, if they are available. In neighborhoods where city residents feel little trust in institutional authorities, mothers may
decide to respond to a violent incident in a way that is consistent

with the culture of the code. For example, when Shante's mom learned that her daughter had been hit with a brick, she and a friend drove to the home of the attacker and sat outside the house in the parked car, "just waiting for her." Recounting the story, Shante's mom says, "You have no idea what was going through my mind." She tells me that if she had taken action that day, whatever she would have done would have been far worse than what the girl did to Shante. She acknowledges that handling the situation with violence is not necessarily the example she would like to set for her daughter. But, she explains, "at times like this" when someone wants to "intimidate" her daughter, she feels she would be justified in going to the girl's house to intimidate *her*. Shante's mom also says that although she wanted to handle the situation the right way, she also wanted Shante to be able to walk through the neighborhood without fear of another attack.

Eventually, Shante's mom decided to press charges against the young woman who had attacked her daughter, an action that Shante initially protested. "They [her mother and the police] asked me if I wanted to press charges. They don't understand that that's not really what I wanted to do . . . I wanted to go around and hurt this girl." Later, she reconsidered, thinking, "Maybe if I do it this way [let the law handle it] something will happen." Shante's mom both models and echoes this sentiment, explaining to Shante's counselors, and me, "We're trying to let the law deal with it." She reaches this decision despite the fact that, like many inner-city residents, she is frequently frustrated by how local law enforcement deals with problems. She says that she tells Shante that even though the law is slow and may not handle the attack the way the family might want, they have to accept that that is how it is. For Shante's mom, who has also served time in prison, the consequences of confronting the girl herself would likely outweigh the benefits. "I've been to prison . . . I ain't afraid of prison," she tells me. "But I don't want to lose my life again. I don't want her to not have a mother."

The police picked up, briefly detained, and then released the teenaged girl who hit Shante with a brick. The girl then returned to the neighborhood, leaving Shante on her own to negotiate future confrontations with her. Already, the two have met again and "almost got into a fight," Shante says. In that instance, Shante and her girlfriend were walking down the street with her girlfriend's baby when Shante saw the girl. The girl, in turn, saw her and "said something," and then Shante's friend "said something" back. The girl advised Shante's friend: "You better watch out before you get the same thing that your friend got," referring to the assault. Shante and her friend considered fighting the girl, but they hesitated because the girl also had a baby with her. Shante telephoned her mother immediately after this confrontation. Shante's mother then called on Shante's father and brother to go and escort them home.

A year after her injury, Shante and I spoke about her decision to let the law handle it. Nothing happened, she tells me. "Yeah, I don't see what they handled, if you asked me. I thought that was attempted murder or something, or attempted assault or something?" she asks, looking to me for confirmation. "Ain't that something?" she says as she shakes her head left to right. When I ask Shante if she still thinks about the incident, she explains, "Like, if I'm walking past where it happened at, like if I walk past there, and it's like me and my friend, I be like, 'Damn, man, that's just where I got hit in the head with the brick at.'" Sometimes, she tries to cope by making light of the event. "I like, try to rewind it to make jokes of it, to make fun of it. I only think about it if I walk past there." Even now, a year later, Shante must consciously manage her interactions with this young woman in order to avoid additional conflict: "Like there's plenty of times I walk and she walk right in front of me [Shante gets up to demonstrate]. Or I walk and she'll walk ahead of me . . . sometimes I be wanting to do it [fight her], then I be like [she takes a deep breath], 'Just go ahead home and just let it be. Just go home and just let it be.'"

"What makes you decide to do that?" I ask.

"Cause it won't—look, if you keep going back at somebody, it won't solve [anything]. It will leave somebody dead and somebody in jail. Violence is not going to lead nowhere."

Her family's intimate experience with the criminal justice system has made Shante acutely aware of the potential consequences of resorting to violence. She explains, "Yeah, I used to think, 'Yeah, I'm going to blow this heifer.' 'I'm going to go get this.' 'I'm going to do that.' That ain't going to do nothing but leave me in the Juvenile Study Center [the city's juvenile jail] or up to LPS [one of two women's prisons in the state] somewhere . . . I'm not willing to sit up in no jail cell . . . telling somebody when to go to sleep, when to eat. No." Shante, like many other inner-city girls, envisions better life possibilities for herself. "That ain't, that is not going to lead me somewhere, and I am not willing to throw my life away," she tells me. "I'm sixteen. I still got a whole life ahead of me and, no, I'm not willing to throw it away—not for something that dumb. 'Cause she hit me in the head with the brick. So, no . . . I just go ahead home and do what I was about to do."

Shante's commitment to nonviolence in all future confrontations is undermined, however, by her perception of the criminal justice system as ineffectual, apathetic, and potentially racist. When I ask her whether, if she were hit on the head with a brick today, she would call on the law to "handle it," Shante responds quickly and emphatically. "No! I would not press charges. No! The district, they don't do nothing." She continues, "It's been almost a year and a week." Then, "No," she corrects herself, after stopping to think for a moment, "a year and three days. So, what have they done?" she asks and immediately supplies the answer: "Nothing." I ask Shante why she thinks the police responded the way they did. She offers a racialized critique of the criminal justice system: "Because they [the police] see it as Black-on-Black crime. So they're not going to do nothing. I done already seen that." So, I question, if she were to be attacked again, what would she do? Shante does not hesitate before replying, "I would have to go and beat her up."

Shante's perception of the criminal justice system, and particularly the police, has been informed not only by her personal experience with the detectives working her case, but also by her direct observation of police interactions with other neighborhood residents. Shante and her neighbors watched as a young Black man from the neighborhood was shot in the head and killed. Describing this violent episode, which had occurred only a few weeks earlier, she recalls, "It was a Sunday and I heard these boys arguing." The argument escalated quickly: "I just saw the boy get his head . . . I just seen him get shot."

Witnessing the shooting made Shante "feel bad," she says, but it also made her angry at what she perceives as widespread indifference to violent acts when they occur in neighborhoods like hers. This indifference is, according to Shante, directly related to racism: "Let this [shooting] happen in a White person's neighborhood, they would have been found that boy who shot that boy in the head. But since they [the police] see it as Black-on-Black crime, they're not going to do nothing. Because they seen two Black, African Americans, fighting." Shante points out that she is merely stating facts, not engaging in reverse racism:

> And it's not a racial thing with me 'cause let me tell you, I got [racially] mixed people in my family. Matter of fact, I'm about to have my mixed nephew, that's mixed with Black and Puerto Rican, so it's not a racial thing. But . . . like they had that boy that had got jumped in the Northeast [a predominantly White, working-to-middle-class area of

the city]. They had that White boy on the news when a couple of Black boys do it [seriously injured him in a fight]. But let that had been Martin Luther King High, let that had been a couple of Black boys, they wouldn't have put that on the news.

Shante also considers the slow response from the ambulance and the police when the young Black man in her neighborhood was shot as evidence of the indifference to, and disregard for, Black life and Black bodies:

> The cops came before the ambulance did. They just threw him in the back of the car. They didn't put him in the back of the car—they *threw* him in the back of the car. He was already dead before he hit the ground, so why would ya'll even rush there—like ya'll was going to rush that man to the hospital? He was dead. And then how the ambulance . . . how the cops going to show up before the ambulance there? That was a White person—that White person would have survived. He would have been all on the news. He would have been all just jolly and joe [happy]. But no, that Black boy had to die.

The kind of distrustful relationship between neighborhood residents and the police that Shante's remarks make clear is a key reason why many cases go unsolved. She is critical of both the police and of neighborhood residents who do "nothing," in her words, to combat the violence that characterizes much of inner-city life, but it is only the residents' lack of action that she finds understandable. Residents resist assisting the police with investigations (labeled on the street as snitching) not only because of a fear of retaliation from assailants but also because of a fear that the police will turn on people who provide information. So while Shante is deeply troubled by the violent crime she witnessed, and wants those responsible punished, she also understands why potential informants do not help police. She would not cooperate either if she knew who did it, she comments.

"I wouldn't," she says, "I mean people would think this would be wrong. To me, I think it would be wrong, too. But, if I knew who killed that boy, I wouldn't have told the cops. No, I wouldn't have told the cops."

"Why not?" I question.

"Because. The cops wouldn't be coming to question me. Talking about some [she trails off]. No, they won't be taking me to jail, interrogating me, no. They would not witness me to no crime so soon as they can't find the person who did it, they can blame it all on me. I seen that happen to people before. No."

"Really?" I press, "You seen that happen to people before?"

"Yeah," Shante confirms. "No, it will not happen to me. I'll have a picture or something. I'll tell somebody else to do it, but I wouldn't do it. No." She pauses for a moment before announcing, "I don't even like cops."

Shante's observations of police and citizen interactions, as well as her own personal experience with the police, shape her understanding of the reliable resources available for negotiating conflict and responding to violence in her neighborhood. While once willing to let the law handle it, her experiences over the past year changed her perspective. Shante is reluctant to let her mother handle it her way for fear that she might return to prison; she learned that she cannot trust the cops because when she gave them a chance they did nothing; and she drew the logical conclusion that she is primarily responsible for her well-being: "I would have to go and beat her up."

Shante's narrative is but one example of how everyday experiences in distressed urban neighborhoods lead African American, inner-city girls to develop the same sort of adversarial attitude toward the police that is typical of young and poor

Black men. Shante's experience informs her critical analysis of the relationship between the criminal justice system, race, and racism in her predominantly Black and low-income, inner-city neighborhood. Shante's experiences also expose a fundamental flaw in the relationship between inner-city residents and the police. Young women may want to call on the police to ensure their own safety, just as people in other social locations do, but they know that doing so in their social world carries many risks. This is how a large number of inner-city youth—including girls—come to believe that the police are not there to protect them (Anderson 1999). Too many girls like Shante conclude that the law does not work for them or their neighbors because neither the police nor the legal system as a whole values the lives of Black people. Within this context, adolescent inner-city girls learn the importance of using a set of personal resources to negotiate conflict and violence in everyday life. In other words, these adolescent girls, like their male counterparts, become socialized into the code of the street.

CHAPTER 2

"It's Not Where You Live, It's How You Live"

WHEN GOOD GIRLS FIGHT

ON A WARM SUMMER DAY, I sit on the stoop outside a South Philadelphia row house with Takeya, a thirteen-year-old girl, who is slim and light-skinned.[1] I ask her if she has been in any recent fights with other girls.

"I'm not in no fights. I'm a good girl," she earnestly replies.

"You're a good girl?" I ask.

"Yeah, I'm a good girl, and I'm-a be a pretty girl at eighteen," she adds confidently.

Takeya's straightened, shoulder-length hair is pulled back carefully into a ponytail and she is neatly dressed in shorts and a T-shirt. Takeya's aura of youthful simplicity and her reserved demeanor are hard to reconcile with what I know about recent events in her life. A neighborhood girl attacked her cousin, also a teenaged girl, in the neck with a knife. The wound required emergency care at the local hospital. The young woman who cut her cousin is "going to jail for attempted murder," Takeya tells me.

Shortly after the knifing, some of Takeya's cousins and family friends stopped by her row home to recruit her to take part in a retaliatory battle, but she resisted their efforts. "I don't fight," she insisted. This is how she recounts the recent episode for me: "They [her cousins and some friends] do, but I don't fight. Like my cousins and them came in here . . . saying give me this and give me that [a reference to an unspecified weapon]. I said, 'No! No. I'm not doing it 'cause y'all are gonna go to jail yourselves.' I said [in response to a detailed recitation of the plans for payback], 'Well, that's you, that ain't me.'" Near the end of our interview, however, Takeya goes out of her way to make sure that I do not leave with a mistaken impression of her street skills. She flatly dismisses the notion that good girls never fight: "I don't want you to think I don't know how to fight," she tells me, "I mean everybody always come get me [for fights]. [I'm] the number one [person they come to get]."

In this conversation, Takeya, like many of the adolescent girls I spoke to about their experiences with interpersonal violence, reveals her commitment to seemingly competing and contradictory goals. She wants to be a good and a pretty girl, yet she also wants to be known as an able fighter—specifically, as "the number one person" people come to for backup. For girls like Takeya, a commitment to an idealized gender identity, such as a good girl, does not necessarily exclude a commitment to being known as an able fighter.

The distinct gender dichotomy that orders much of social relations in mainstream society is confusingly contradictory for many adolescent girls who come of age in distressed urban areas. Takeya's desire to be a pretty girl, for example, reflects both stereotypically feminine concerns rooted in mainstream expectations of appropriate femininity and Black respectability. In Takeya's world, beauty is assessed using an intersecting set of expectations that include skin color, hair texture, and body shape. A light-brown complexion, a good perm (professionally, or at least competently, straightened hair, or naturally curly hair, is a positive attribute, as opposed to "kinky" or "nappy" hair, which is generally considered a drawback),[2] and a slim figure help make a teenaged girl pretty. In this context, as Takeya's story makes clear, pretty is often conflated with good, as girls who fight regularly are often physically marked during their battles (Banks 2000; Collins 2004).

Still, being a good girl or a pretty girl is not simply something that one is—it is not a static state. Instead, pretty is an ongoing gendered project that is accomplished during everyday interactions with others on the street and in the home (West and Zimmerman 1987; West and Fenstermaker 1995). Girls' gendered survival projects have as much to do with how girls work the code of the street as they do with any ascribed characteristics they possess. In this chapter, I identify some of the contradictions and dilemmas that emerge for girls like Takeya as they work the code. Takeya's experience, taken with that of several other girls who strive to fit the good girl persona, suggests the difficult gender work involved in inner-city survival.

WHAT MAKES A GIRL GOOD?

Competing images of good and ghetto girls emerge at the intersections of race, gender, class, and sexuality. The essential attributes of the good girl are drawn from various sources, as Patricia Hill Collins explains. Like all women, Black women and girls are evaluated in reference to "multiple others," including White women, "all men, sexual outlaws (prostitutes and lesbians), unmarried women, and girls." Those girls (or women) who are evaluated as good during their interactions with peers, family members, or other adults generally come closer to meeting the expectations of "a hegemonic (White) femininity" that "relegates Black women to the bottom of the gender hierarchy" (Collins 2004, 193). Girls who want to grow up to be respectable Black ladies, then, must manage their interactions and gender displays in ways that mirror mainstream notions of appropriate femininity and challenge stereotypical notions of Black femininity. In this way, girls are evaluated as good (or not) at least as much in terms of who she *is not* as who she is. Good girls do not look or act like men or boys. Good girls do not run wild in the streets; instead, they spend the majority of their time in controlled settings: family, school, home, or church. Good girls are appropriately deferential to the men in their lives. Good girls are not sexually promiscuous, nor are they anything other than heterosexual. Good girls grow up to be ladies and once they have achieved this special-status position they become committed to putting the needs of their family first.

Teenaged girls also construct their gender identity in reference to various media images. Since the 1980s, hip-hop culture, in particular, has become a major socializing influence on young Black girls (Collins 2004). Adolescents like Takeya draw on definitions of femininity embedded in popular songs, music videos, and other media (George 1998; Dyson 2001; Cole and Guy-Sheftall 2003; Rose 1994). Hip-hop images of women—bitches and hos, gold diggers, hoodrats, ghetto chicks, ride-or-die bitches, as they are called in a number of popular rap songs— exploit traditional understandings about a woman's place while also reinforcing racialized ideas about Black women, girls, boys, and men, and their relationship to one another. These images of Black masculinity and femininity have a distinct hold on young Black women (Sharpley-Whiting 2007) and teenaged girls consume, internalize, and respond to these images, and others, as they work to define what it means to be a good girl in today's inner city.[3] The images of Black femininity that are popularized in hip-hop culture shape girls' understanding of the resources that are available to them, influence how they interact with their peers, and inform how they evaluate themselves. Will they (can they?) maintain an appropriate feminine demeanor (i.e., not be loud, aggressive, rude, or pushy), one that will successfully distinguish them from all men in general, and from Black men in particular? Will they (can they?) demonstrate an appropriate level of deference toward the men in their lives? Will they (can they?) remain sexually conservative, heterosexual, and not a freak or a ho?[4]

Among the girls I interviewed, those who seemed most interested in crafting a respectable identity usually—but not always—came from families that were invested in being seen by others as respectable, principled, or decent. These families included those without a traditional two-parent family structure who were still striving for decency (Anderson 1999; Richie 1996). During a visit I made to the South Philadelphia home of Ms. Rose, a mother of three and grandmother of five who very much values her family's good reputation, she clarified the distinction between a street kid and a good girl in the following excerpt from my field notes:

> I have just finished an hour-long conversation with Lacy, one of Ms. Rose's two teenaged granddaughters. Ms. Rose is walking me the short distance across the front room of her row home to the front door. This walk, which should have taken no more than a few seconds, lasts nearly thirty minutes. Ms. Rose wants to share with me what she sees as important information. As we begin moving slowly toward the front door, she points towards her other teenaged granddaughter, a slightly overweight, light-skinned girl. This young woman has been sitting quietly in a corner of the living room, next to a lamp, with her head nearly buried in a textbook since I first entered the house. Ms. Rose explains to me how this granddaughter is different from some of the other teenaged girls in the neighborhood: "She's not a street kid . . . she stays in the house." She continues, now comparing this granddaughter to an older granddaughter who no longer lives at home. "She's like my other granddaughter," Ms. Rose confides. "She would always be in the house around the older women. You would always see her sitting with her head in her hands, just listening." I nod my head encouragingly and the story continues. "She went to state university. She's married now to a good man. They're not

out there running around and she's still going back for more school." At the end of this explanation, Ms. Rose's granddaughter looks up, offers a shy smile, and then bows her head over her textbook once again.

Ms. Rose's description of these two granddaughters illustrates a belief common among mothers and grandmothers who are charged with raising children in the inner city: good girls who stay off the street, who do well in school, have the best chance of staying out of trouble and of eventually getting out of the dangerous neighborhood. This belief stands in contrast to the discouraging life chances of urban, adolescent boys, who are often written off early on in their lives as bad boys (Ferguson 2000). In these school settings, especially within public schools that are hypersensitive to the disciplinary breaches of adolescent boys, good girls can enact a form of femininity that brings them benefits. By embracing and enacting mainstream and Black middle-class gendered expectations while at school, girls may receive positive attention from teachers and other social rewards. Generally, girls run into trouble with school authorities only when they fail to meet the expected standards of femininity.

Peers' reactions to good girls' strategies at school, however, may be significantly less positive. Especially among peers who are invested in crafting their own identities as fighters, the good girl who receives positive attention from others, including teachers and boys, is often derided as thinking she is "all that." The good girl, particularly if she is light-skinned and has good hair, is perceived as arrogant, as thinking she is better than other girls. The good girl rarely accepts this perception of herself as valid. She may be cognizant of meeting feminine expectations of beauty, and proud of her style, but this, she protests, does not mean that she thinks she's all that. From her perspective, it is jealousy that fuels her peers' misperceptions of her. According to the good girl, girl fighters often lack the physical attributes valued as pretty or beautiful and express their resentment with their she-thinks-she's-all-that dismissal. This resentment fuels the desire to mark the faces of pretty girls during battles—to permanently diminish the basis for their special-status position in school and neighborhood settings.[5]

The pretty girl whose identity is invested primarily in her looks and the girl fighter whose identity is invested primarily in her actions are locked in a relationship that is based on a very old racialized and gendered hierarchy. Each girl may, in fact, want the same thing: an identity that brings with it a sense of personal power, self-esteem, and the respect of others. Because each one needs the other in order to maintain her reputation, however, the two seem to be always at odds. Their routine and ritualized physical and verbal battles reinforce the internalized racial hierarchy that is produced and reproduced through girls' everyday evaluations of themselves and others. The pretty girls are treated as if they are better or more special than other girls. Those girls who challenge normative expectations of gender and possess physical attributes that are devalued or ignored may eventually become frustrated by the less positive treatment they receive from others, including teachers, family members, and peers. Over time, the gulf between the good girl and the girl fighter widens and tensions spill over into actions such as bumps or stares in the hallways as the girls move between classrooms. These interactions, in turn, may escalate into a physical fight. The superficial justifications—she's jealous or she thinks she's all that—mask the racialized and gendered hierarchy of feminine beauty that divides young Black women into good girls and ghetto girls.[6]

SITUATED SURVIVAL STRATEGIES

As urban, adolescent girls navigate the difficult and often unpredictable inner-city terrain, they develop a set of what I describe as *situated survival strategies*: patterned forms of interpersonal interaction, and routine or ritualized activities oriented around a concern for securing their personal well-being.[7] The knowledge of threats to their safety shapes their daily lives. Urban, adolescent girls craft their situated survival strategies within the context of inner-city life, and between the extreme and oftentimes unrealistic physical and behavioral expectations of the good African American girl, who will grow up to be a respectable Black lady, and the behavioral expectations of the code, which encourages the adoption of aggressive postures or behaviors that are typically expected of boys and men, yet are essential to managing threats in this context. Girls' development of an individualized survival strategy is interwoven into her development as an adolescent girl. The good girl who survives inner-city life must simultaneously act like a girl and be ready to physically defend herself when necessary. The girl who is more deeply invested in presenting a public identity as a fighter feels similar cultural pressure, and also adapts to these circumstances, albeit in ways that make her vulnerable to negative evaluations and subsequent formal and informal punishments.

In developing the situated survival strategy that works best for her, the inner-city girl draws on a set of personal resources, such as ascribed characteristics, acquired status, physical ability, and personality traits. For example, a girl who is aware that her skin tone or hair texture make her pretty, giving her a special-status position in her family and among her peers, may actively avoid the physical battles that can result in cuts and scratches to her face, a common effect of physical fights among girls. In turn, a girl who is more confident in her fighting ability, and whose physical characteristics may have already marked her as an outsider, may actively eschew the constraints of mainstream gender ideals for the perceived rewards that come along with fighting and winning.

Generally, girls who fight only rarely are more apt to be described as good girls; these girls are quick to distinguish themselves from girls who fight more frequently. Nevertheless, the amount of energy these girls invest in *not* fighting, typically by actively avoiding those places and interactions that might lead to physical battles, seemed to me to be no less than what fighters expend seeking out opportunities to prove their abilities. I call the two common strategies teenaged girls use to reduce the likelihood of encountering serious threats to their well-being on the streets or in school settings *situational avoidance* and *relational isolation*.

The concept of situational avoidance captures all of the work teenaged girls do to avoid social settings that pose threats to their well-being and situations in which potential conflicts might arise. In contrast to girl fighters, who feel confident spending time on the street and in places where others hang out (what Anderson [1999] terms "staging areas"), situational avoiders confine themselves to the home, spending the majority of their time reading books, doing schoolwork, watching television, or daydreaming about being somewhere—anywhere—other than in their homes or neighborhoods. When they are outside, the same girls will rely on their own mental maps of areas and people to avoid. They restrict their movement in public spaces; they are reluctant to explore new areas of the city or to alter their daily routines outside their home in any significant way. In the most serious cases, girls who have had repeated conflicts at school may avoid going to school altogether, choosing to remove themselves from the place where fights are most likely to occur.

The concept of *relational isolation* illuminates the work girls do to isolate themselves from close friendships, especially those with other young women. The ties of loyalty and affection that accompany friendships increase the likelihood that girls will come to the defense of one another, if the need arises. Thus, by avoiding close friendships, girls can reduce the likelihood of their involvement in a physical conflict. Among the teenaged girls I spoke with, the most common strategy was to divide relationships with other girls into two categories: friends and associates. Often, when I asked girls about their friends, they would correct me, pointing out, "I don't have friends. I got associates." In settings governed by the culture of the code, friends and associates connote two distinct status positions, which in turn reflect one person's degree of loyalty to another. Friend indicates a strong loyalty link; associate indicates a weaker link. Generally, it is expected that you will fight for a friend, but there is no equivalent requirement to fight for an associate. Designating other members of one's peer group or social network as associates instead of friends thus limits the likelihood of becoming involved in interpersonal conflicts on the grounds of loyalty. This strategy of insulating themselves from potential conflicts by limiting the strength of their social relationships may have serious long-term consequences for inner-city girls. Girls are deliberately stunting the growth of their relational networks at a stage in adolescent development typically associated with the creation of healthy, trusting, and loving relationships. The way the culture of the code of the street alters patterns of adolescent development may be particularly significant for young girls, who are generally believed to be more relational-based than young men.[8]

In addition to their negative effects on girls' emotional and psychological development, these strategies can also work to make girls more physically vulnerable, since intense peer relationships can be protective. In the culture of the code, friends are *worth* fighting for. If you forge relationships that never require you to come to the defense of another, then who will defend you when you need help? What does a good girl who repeatedly isolates herself from potentially troubling people and places do when she finds she has to fight? Kailee's experiences, described below, illustrate some of the limits of the strategies used by girls to avoid potential conflicts, and also identify conditions under which a girl can fight and still be evaluated by family members and others as generally good.

THE LIMITS OF SITUATIONAL
AVOIDANCE: KAILEE'S STORY

Kailee, an eighth-grader who lives with her aunt and legal guardian, Ms. White, has been the target of another young woman's challenges for the duration of the school year. Ms. White has been consumed with attempts to resolve this situation. She tells me that other students in the school don't like Kailee or her younger brother because they are "different," she says. Both children have light skin and Ms. White suspects that other young women in particular target Kailee because schoolboys often perceive her different physical characteristics as desirable. Kailee and her brother further display their difference through their style of dress. Kailee's brother, for example, wears a pair of fitted jeans rather than the more commonly favored baggy style. And Kailee, in contrast to some adolescent girls who work to craft fashionable styles of dress that make them stand out, prefers a self-imposed uniform that consists of a slightly oversized, white button-down shirt that hides her developed figure, a pair of loose blue Capri pants, and new, plain white Reeboks.

As Kailee sits quietly by, Ms. White repeats a sample of the verbal assaults her niece is subjected to by her peers. Ridiculing her long brown hair, they suggest, "Why don't you cut your hair?" In reference to Kailee's seemingly blemish-free face, they taunt, "You got a mustache." She has been told she has a "pointy nose."

"The list goes on," Ms. White says. These are nasty jibes intended to challenge the special status that these physical attributes accord Kailee, and their daily repetition makes them all the more demoralizing. It is not the verbal assaults alone, however, that have so involved Ms. White, nor are they the chief reason Kailee's school life has become nearly intolerable.

One of Kailee's classmates is explicit in her intent to do her harm. Ms. White has taken to driving her niece to and from school in order to protect Kailee. On one recent afternoon, even as Ms. White was ushering Kailee into her car for the short drive home, this adolescent girl approached the car, screaming, "I'ma get you! I'ma get you!" at Kailee. According to her aunt, the steady stream of verbal assaults and physical threats has left Kailee socially isolated and depressed. This prompted Ms. White to send her niece to counseling midway through the school year. After several months of sessions, Kailee recently completed her last visit; in her aunt's opinion, she seems a little better. Still, Ms. White remains concerned because Kailee has, she says, "no friends, not one."

At this point, Kailee breaks her silence. "Yes, I do," she interrupts, staring directly at her aunt, who is sitting across the room. "I have you."

Ms. White is aware that she provides a great deal of emotional support for Kailee. She is also aware of the limits of her ability to protect her niece from the ongoing threats to her physical and emotional well-being at school. Kailee's situation presents her aunt with a difficult dilemma. Ms. White is a veteran of the inner city; in fact, she grew up in the same neighborhood where she now lives. She comes from what she describes as a "fighting family." Her brother, Kailee's father, is a drug dealer, well known in the neighborhood, who is no stranger to violence ("He turned around and shot somebody with a shotgun!"). Ms. White, though, has embraced what she calls "Christian values," which lead her to reject violence as a solution to life's problems. Further, she is committed to teaching that lesson to the children under her charge: "I'm trying to teach them that they don't have to solve situations that way." Still, modeling nonviolence is difficult for Ms. White, especially when other women directly challenge her. For example, she admitted that when she was told that the mother of the girl who has been challenging Kailee was "looking for her," her response was to ask, defiantly, "Where she at?" Another time, while Ms. White was visiting with school officials, the mother of a different girl who was also taunting Kailee came into the office and physically threatened Ms. White. As she recounts the story, Ms. White physically reenacts her response to this challenge. She lifts her shoulders up and back and simultaneously raises her chest and her eyebrows as she repeats her response to this would-be assailant: "Now, you really think I'm going to let you do that? Do you really think that?" When Ms. White hears from other neighborhood residents that the girl who is challenging Kailee is going to get her family members involved, Ms. White asks, "Do you know who I can get?" She explains that someone in her network already has come to her to ask if she needed help with the situation, and that if she had said yes, "that would have been it." However, Ms. White recognizes that to handle the situation with violence, without first trying nonviolent strategies, would contradict her Christian values and undermine the model she is trying to provide for Kailee and her brother. Instead, Ms. White has committed herself to instructing Kailee to avoid physical conflict if at all possible. "First, tell someone," she instructs Kailee, and then, "if you have to," fight.

Despite Kailee's love for her aunt and respect for the lessons she is trying to teach her and her brother, she eventually resolved to address the problem her own way. She had grown tired of the constant assaults and, particularly, of repeatedly being deferential toward her challenger. At school recently, she decided, on the spur of the moment, to fight back. Kailee encountered the young woman who so often said she was going to "get" her while she was running from the playground into one of the school entrances. This time, instead of moving out of the girl's way and murmuring a soft, deferential "'scuse me," Kailee took the offensive. She directed the other girl to "watch where you going." This direct challenge quickly escalated into a shoving match, and then a fight. Once the fight was broken up, both young women were suspended.

Since this incident, Ms. White has continued to provide Kailee with emotional support. She did not punish her niece for fighting, and she has not activated her network resources to prepare for retaliation. In keeping with her values, she has not encouraged Kailee to consider retaliation either. Being a Christian provides Ms. White with an alternative framework for operating in what she knows to be a violent world. However, she is also aware that absolute adherence to nonviolence, while encouraged by her faith, may not be realistic in everyday inner-city life. As a result, she allows for some give-and-take between her beliefs and the behaviors she accepts as necessary for preserving basic personal security in her own life and in the lives of the children in her care.

Kailee's story illustrates the dilemmas that face girls who try to be good while still held accountable to the more street-oriented elements that form the foundation of the culture of the code. Her experiences also underscore the advantages and disadvantages that accompany the special-status position accorded to girls whose physical attributes more closely mirror mainstream expectations of femininity. The limits of the strategies used by girls who do not see themselves as fighters to avoid potential conflicts also reveal a set of conditions under which a good girl can fight and still be considered good. In these circumstances, girls like Kailee meet mainstream expectations for acceptable feminine behavior by demonstrating restraint (e.g., she spends the school year trying to physically avoid her main challenger and she is consistently deferential in situations where she cannot avoid contact) and she also maintains a level of respectability by fighting only when she has reached a reasonable limit. She pushes against, but stops short of breaking, the frame of respectable femininity in this setting.

Like Takeya and Kailee, Danielle's story, which is featured in the following pages, also reveals how girls manage the competing expectations that accompany their working of the code.

Like other girls, Danielle is also concerned with maintaining a hold on the rewards and resources that are provided to girls who more closely fit mainstream and local expectations regarding femininity. Her story reveals how, over the course of her teenaged years, she developed a set of strategies that allowed her to manage potential challenges from others without sacrificing all claims to respectability.

A GOOD GIRL FROM THE PROJECTS: DANIELLE'S STORY

Urban, adolescent girls in distressed inner-city neighborhoods negotiate for respect, space, and security against a backdrop of subtle and not-so-subtle violence. Danielle's narrative highlights how even those who are skilled at navigating potential threats of violence in their immediate surroundings may become involved in physical conflicts as a consequence of their necessary interaction with the code. Danielle's story also reveals the work that a girl must engage in to avoid interpersonal battles, as well as the limitations of these strategies.

Danielle is a slim, medium brown–skinned young woman with a bright smile framed by cheeks that make her look younger than she is and eyes that make her look older than her nineteen years. She is a recent graduate of one of the city's public high schools—the first in her immediate family to earn a high school diploma. Danielle has lived in the same housing project apartment for all but the previous year of her life. She ran track for her high school team and performed well enough academically to be admitted to a small, predominantly White university. The school was hours and worlds away from her inner-city home, Danielle says. Life on the university campus, set in a mostly rural area in the western region of Pennsylvania, presented Danielle with startling contrasts to her hometown experiences.

Danielle enjoyed her time at the university, but left school in the middle of her freshman year after discovering that she was several weeks pregnant. Her baby's father, who was attending the same university on a partial athletic scholarship, also dropped out and has returned to an inner-city neighborhood across town from Danielle's. Since his return, he has taken a job at a local department store and calls and visits Danielle often. While she is excited about having a baby and, as her boyfriend has promised repeatedly, making a family, she is also regretful about being "back here," in the project apartment where she grew up. "When I left," she tells me, "I didn't plan on coming back, except for holidays and stuff like that."

Danielle now spends most days in the twelfth-floor apartment she shares with her mother and two brothers, a nine-year-old and an energetic eleven-month-old. Danielle's grandmother and grandfather live several floors below and Danielle visits them often. Together, this group of family members provides Danielle with a support system. She relies on her Christian faith for support, as well. Once the baby is born, Danielle plans to move into an apartment a few floors below her mother's unit. Her mother, who has maintained cordial relationships with various housing authority officials over the last eighteen years, negotiated this fortunate move. While much of Danielle's time is spent imagining what life will be like when her baby arrives, our conversations about life in the projects and about her general and personal experiences with violence highlight the complicated backdrop of insecurity that informs her everyday life. Even young women like Danielle, who do not identify as "fighters," must still confront and negotiate threats of violence.

Over the last several years, Philadelphia has implemented a series of urban redevelopment initiatives. These often have involved moving housing-complex residents out of their existing homes, destroying these recently vacated buildings, and relocating the residents in other forms of housing. The city's landscape is now marked by at least three distinct types of housing projects. There are low-rise complexes that stand only two stories high and are laid out in an isolating pattern of short, dead-end streets. Some of these complexes resemble medium-security prisons: police survey the exterior while residents freely move about the interior. There are also new housing developments, often only a few stories high, built to replace housing stock that has been torn down. Finally, a handful of high-rise housing projects remain, thus far undisturbed by the city's housing restructuring-via-demolition program, which in some areas has reduced whole blocks to nothing more than rubble. Danielle lives in one of these few remaining high-rise complexes.

At the entrance to Danielle's complex is a sign: "New Village Apartments." The country design of the sign provides an ironic, if unintended, contrast to the massive concrete, brick, and steel structures that loom behind it. A winding road leads into a parking lot at the heart of the complex. Even a hurried look around confirms that this is no ordinary high-rise. Each of the three identical buildings is well-worn. The balconies attached to the exterior of the apartments are enclosed in black wire cages. Small children peek out from behind the wire like captive birds. On one side of the parking lot sits a brightly colored play area, but there is no sign of children at play. A few hundred feet from the entrance to the buildings are the remnants of a tennis court. Weeds shoot up from all sides of the space where the nets should be. The ten-foot-high metal fence around the court makes it appear imprisoned. On the far side of the court, a small hill is visible. During the summer, the voices of young children at the nearby public pool carry over the hill into the complex. Construction work is being done in front of Danielle's building. It is unclear exactly what the goal is, but a big ditch is being dug from one apartment unit to the next. Two White construction workers walk by as I move through the work area. Two identical play areas sit on either side of the project complex. Instead of the protective ground cover of sand or wood chips typically found under children's play structures, the ground in these play areas is, like almost everything else in the complex, made of concrete.

In contrast to the city streets and neighborhoods I have been visiting, where the sight and sounds of children are more common, here I see no children in the play areas. In fact, even during the day, there are very few children in sight anywhere outside. The isolating design of this project housing makes it difficult for caretakers to keep an eye on children while they play, and the potential for violence precludes leaving children unattended. Young children who do play outside often must share space with others involved in more adult activities. For example, there are usually a few teenaged boys who just hang out, seated on one of the benches that lead in a straight line from the parking lot to the third unit in the housing complex. Occasionally, I notice an individual woman, sometimes dressed, like the young men, in the long white T-shirts that are currently a staple of the young urban male wardrobe, join the group. Sometimes, the activities older kids pursue are more problematic. On one daytime visit to Danielle's home, for instance, I passed a young boy and girl, neither more than ten years old, shooting balls at a portable basketball hoop set up outside the playground area. "Don't hang on it!" the boy pleads with his female playmate. "You're going to break it," he predicts as she continues to hang, stone-faced, from the rim of the kid-sized hoop. Stepping just beyond this scene, I walk into a wafting cloud of marijuana smoke. Looking around, trying to locate the source of the odor, I see a group of young men in their twenties crowded around a car in the parking lot. A huge puff of white smoke is drifting upward and disappearing above their heads.

The weed-smoking teens and the hoop-shooting youngsters are not more than fifteen yards apart.

The ground-floor entrance to Danielle's apartment building is typical of project housing, a physical testament to the threat of violence that forms the backdrop of residents' daily lives. A thick piece of clear plastic, a material almost identical to the barriers that separate vendors from customers in the many take-out food stores that crowd the corners of the surrounding neighborhood, forms a wall between the outer and inner doors of the building. Usually, a Philadelphia Housing Authority guard sits at a counter behind the acrylic barrier. (Sometimes, there is no guard on duty and the door, deliberately left slightly ajar, buzzes steadily. Young people from adjacent buildings are especially pleased to find the door unsecured because this allows them to skirt the security measures that restrict residents of other housing units from freely entering buildings in which they do not live.) On my first visit to Danielle's building, the guard on duty is a brown-skinned woman whose salt and pepper hair, pulled back into a neat bun, suggests that she is somewhere in her midforties. As I approach the door, unsure of how to proceed, I glance at the guard behind the acrylic shield and then look at the intercom box that hangs on the wall between her post and the thick metal door of the housing complex.

The guard yells from behind the plastic, "What apartment?"

"Twelve-sixty," I say.

"Hit the number and then the pound sign," she instructs, still yelling.

I follow her directions, pressing each button with careful firmness. A moment after pressing the last button, the sound of a phone ringing comes over the intercom. Danielle answers the phone.

"It's Nikki," I tell her and she buzzes me in. I open and walk through the thick metal door, only to find another metal door. When I open and step through this second door, I find myself in a small, cool lobby, where I am greeted by an underlying scent of stale air and urine.

I take the elevator up to the twelfth floor, step out, and make a quick left. As I pass the door to the stairway, I consider using the stairs as an alternate route on my way out. Then I quickly reconsider, as I weigh the risks—stories of young girls being assaulted in stairwells circulate among residents of the projects. This is a one-time decision for me; if I lived here, though, considerations like this one would shape my personal choices on a daily basis. I think about this as I continue to walk down the hallway. Every apartment door is the same shade of green, and every door is closed, except the one adjacent to Danielle's. This door, which has an "All for Islam" bumper sticker affixed to it, is nearly halfway ajar, allowing the Middle Eastern music playing deep inside the apartment to spill out into the hallway. I knock on Danielle's door, and after a moment, I hear her undo the lock. She opens the door and stands in the doorway, her baby brother on her hip, her hair slightly messy, and her face lit with a big smile. She has gained some weight since I saw her last. The baby that was hardly more than a thought when we spoke months ago now declares its existence, an unmistakable bulge in the middle of Danielle's otherwise slender frame.

"Hi!" she says. "Come on in."

Violence as the Backdrop of Everyday Life

During our first visit, I asked Danielle how she liked living in the projects. "It could be better," she responded. "Without the drugs and all, um, the violence that go on like cops and stuff and the fire alarms be going off in the middle of the night like three or four in the morning because some kid pulled the alarm. . . . And, um, you know, crack heads that be in the building and stuff like that. Knock on your door asking for stuff. It could be better." On the other hand, she notes that, physically, the apartment building is "better than it was when I was growing up." The tiled flooring of the hallway outside the apartment door, for instance, is a step up from the dull concrete that used to be there. She is wary, though, of the goals of the current construction project: "I think that they are taking down the balconies—they want to keep us in here for real."

The city's latest approach to improvements in public housing has required relocating some of the residents. This has brought together in a single space groups that have been in conflict for years. Danielle explains the situation this way: "You know they tore down projects in other areas and they sent people from those projects here. So now you have three different projects [that] didn't get along to begin with and now they really don't." Not surprisingly, "there's been a lot of fights this summer because of that."

Danielle was recently drawn into a police action in her neighborhood as she walked home from the shopping center. A "Black man" running away from a "White man" dashed across her path. Police cars, sirens howling, were trailing the two runners. They trapped the Black man against a wire fence that began where the elevated train descended into a below-ground tunnel. Sensing no other way out, the man, Danielle tells me, "jumps up the wall [fence]! You wouldn't think he would make it because the wall is high, but he did." She pauses, reflecting on this scene for a moment. "A Black man on the run—if we weren't there, I know they would have shot him. He jumped—the wall caught his shirt, but he made it."

Danielle's nine-year-old brother, who has been hanging out with us in their living room, adds, "It's still there. Yup, it's still there." (I check on my next visit. As I walk by the place where the elevated train drops out of sight, I look up. I can see a blue T-shirt hanging triumphantly from the top of the twelve-foot chain-link fence).

"That was the first time I was up that close," Danielle explains to me excitedly. "I mean, I seen a gun before, but not like that. That was like the movies."

Danielle's most personal and still most memorable experience with violence occurred during her early teen years, when she was dating a young man named Jamal. She discovered inadvertently that he was a local drug dealer: She greeted him with a hug and found that he had a gun tucked in his waistband. That discovery was enough to convince her that she should end the relationship, but Jamal convinced her that her love was extremely important to him, that she was the first woman he ever truly cared about. Against her better judgment, Danielle continued to date Jamal and while doing so encouraged him to make some changes. For example, she got him to limit his dealing to less dangerous drugs—weed, for example, instead of crack. Still, dating a drug dealer, Danielle confides, was difficult. "It was hard, like, we couldn't go anywhere, to the movies or anything because he was selling and you never knew when someone who was looking for him would find him." An episode on a street corner made it clear to Danielle that dating a drug dealer was not just potentially dangerous but actually so:

> Well, one day I wanted to go see him on the block. I wanted to see him because I hadn't seen him in a few days and my cousin was with me and she wanted to see her boyfriend too. But Jamal told me never to come to the corner when he was working. But my cousin and I went to see them and we walked up to him and my cousin's boyfriend. The next thing I remember is this black car with tinted windows pulling up to the corner. As I'm talking to my boyfriend and she is talking to her boyfriend, the next thing I see is a gun pointed at my cousin's head. I'm like frozen. The guy with the gun is asking my cousin's boyfriend where his seven hundred dollars is. He keeps saying, "Where my money?"

After like, forever, my boyfriend reaches into his pocket and pulls out a thick wad, *thick*, he pulls out nine hundred dollars and gives it to the guy. He's like, "Here it is, and here's an extra two hundred dollars. Just take it."

The guy with the gun took the money, got back into the black car, and the car pulled away. The young men left the corner, and Danielle's cousin collapsed. Danielle concludes by explaining why her boyfriend sacrificed his own money, which he would remain accountable for, for her cousin: "He gave him the money because of me, but after that I was like, I can't do this no more, you know. He still calls me to this day, though. When we first broke up he was like, 'If I can't have you, then no one can.' And I was like, 'Oh no, please don't turn into some stalker thing,' you know, but he didn't. Nope, he still calls me, and I tell him what is going on, I'm pregnant, got a boyfriend." Undoubtedly, some young women are attracted by the lifestyle that some drug dealers can afford. But for Danielle, and others like her, the risks associated with dating a drug dealer outweighed any of the potential benefits. Once she realized the extent of the danger dating Jamal exposed her to, Danielle ended the relationship. Moreover, she opted for negotiating the potentially violent setting in which she was growing up by avoiding similar kinds of social relationships in the future.

"IT's How You Live"

"Some people will use living in the projects as an excuse," Danielle observes, "but not me. It's not where you live, it's how you live." As she was growing up, she tried to live peaceably. Danielle was particularly adept at mediating potential conflicts in school before they reached the point of fistfights or worse. She devised strategies that were effective enough to help her avoid fighting throughout almost all of her nineteen years. As we talked, she described three of these strategies. First, she was careful to avoid presenting herself as a person who "had a point to prove," as some young inner-city women do. With nothing to prove and no reputation as a "fighter" to protect, Danielle could manage "not saying nothing." She didn't feel compelled to meet every taunt with a countertaunt, every hallway bump with a push in return. "If people, like, call me names, or push me, or something, I just brush it off. Something like that." When a potential conflict did arise, Danielle turned to a second strategy—she quickly activated her networks of authority. "Or [I would] go to someone, like I talk to a teacher. I was always talking to a teacher." She laughs. "I, um, I'm scared, I'm a punk! [More laughter.] Little punk." Lastly, Danielle was willing to try to talk out potential conflicts before they escalated into public battles. For example, she waited until after school, away from the eyes of an audience, to approach a young woman who had been "talking about her." Cutting through her classmate's tough front, Danielle simply explained, "You don't even know me." The two talked briefly and the next day the young woman told her friends that Danielle was "okay." And that was it.

LOYALTY LINKS

Despite her preference for avoiding or defusing potential conflicts, Danielle acknowledges that some situations require a fight. "I got no point to prove," she explains, "but sometimes you have to [fight] or they'll just punk you all the time." One common way that young women who are not "fighters" nevertheless become involved in fights is through "loyalty links." Social relationships involving individuals who consider themselves "friends" (as opposed to "associates") carry serious reciprocal obligations, including the willingness to fight on behalf of one another. In Danielle's case, her loyalty link to her best friend involved her in the first and (thus far) only fight in her life.

She recounts the background to the conflict this way. For a time while both girls were in high school, Danielle's best friend Katrina lived with Danielle and her family in their project apartment. A group of girls at their school repeatedly threatened to "get" Katrina. Danielle, of course, was very concerned: "It's my best friend and I don't want nobody to hurt her." One afternoon, as Danielle and Katrina began the walk from the high school to the housing project, this group of young women followed them, making it clear that they wanted to fight: "And we were walking and they were following her, calling her names, um, telling her that 'You better watch your back, "B" [bitch], or fight me now,' just sayin' stuff. So, we got in front of [the local hospital] and I said, 'Katrina, drop your bags,' cause they're behind me, and they're coming closer. And I dropped my bags. Just to make sure that nobody not tryin' to jump her."

Although she had no personal experience with fighting, Danielle's inner-city life had taught her "the basics." She knew, for example, that it would be a mistake to keep their backs turned to the other girls since this would invite a sneak attack (i.e., she and Katrina might be "jumped"). Danielle also took a precaution many other young women do when a fight is imminent. Before she and Katrina left school, she had called ahead to alert her mother, who then began to head toward the school. She met the two girls when they were about halfway home. When she arrived, Danielle's mom, although she was several months pregnant, was prepared to do her part to keep the fight from getting out of hand. Danielle describes what happened next: "Katrina got into the street—and this was something— they was about to swing and fight each other. And I, my mom was there and I was there, so we can make sure that nobody don't interfere with their fight. You know, make sure it's not a blood bath or nothing like that, you know, make sure . . .'cause sometimes you got to fight, not fight, but get into that type of battle to let them know that I'm not scared of you and you can't keep harassing me [and] thinking that it's okay."

Almost as soon as Katrina and the young woman she squared off with began to fight, Danielle found herself transformed from bystander to combatant: "I was there like just watching everything, and then before I knew it, I got snuck . . . I got— somebody came and pulled my hair and hit me in the eye. So, I'm, [I] can't see. I'm like, 'What's going on?' I'm tripping over the curb, fallin' on the ground, hit my back on the curb and everything like that. And I'm on the ground, and I'm getting like this girl beating on me and stuff, and I'm like, 'Who is this?' I couldn't really see 'cause my eye got hit, and I'm trying to see who this is, and me and her fighting and everything."

As Danielle regained her bearings, she moved from receiving punches to landing some: "So, I flip her over and I finally get my sight back and we fighting because she hittin' me, I'm hittin' her and everything. Then she get up and I run after her, 'cause I'm real angry. I want to like hurt this girl because she hit me for no reason. So I go up to her [and] me and her fightin' and then they ran. . . . And we was like, 'Come back and finish! Don't run now because you gettin' your butt kicked!' So they left and we got in the car, we came home. My eye was black. I was seeing stars." She laughs.

This experience did not convert Danielle from a good girl into a fighter, but she did admit that she felt good when she went to school the next day. Now she knew with certainty that she was not, after all, "a punk." Some time after this fight, Katrina moved to the South with her family. Danielle returned to her preferred strategy of avoiding conflict. So, for example, if she saw the girls she and Katrina fought with, she would attempt to avoid walking by them or speaking directly to them. She did not encounter any additional problems with any of these young women.

If not for her loyalty link to her best friend, Danielle might have made it through her entire high school career without ever getting into a fight. Some young women undoubtedly do so. The important point here is that inner-city girls who do not end up in fights are not simply lucky, nor are they all "scared little punks," to borrow Danielle's phrase. Instead, these young women are careful strategists who expend time and energy every day negotiating potential threats of interpersonal conflict before they erupt into violent battles. Danielle, for instance, deliberately restricted her social network to a few friends in her neighborhood, her tight-knit family, and family-based connections to a Christian church. At home, she chose to spend most of her time inside the apartment, to avoid being drawn into her neighbors' "petty" arguments, since these disputes could quickly escalate into fights. In school, Danielle used a combination of strategies to avoid or defuse likely confrontations. Her only direct involvement in a fight stemmed from her unwillingness to let anyone "just hurt" her best friend.

Danielle recognized that discovering that she could "hold her own" in a street fight increased her sense of personal confidence. Still, she did not recast herself as a fighter after this battle. She remained a good girl and resumed her conflict avoidance strategies inside and outside school. Because most of the people in her social world recognize the circumstances that surrounded her actions as legitimate grounds for temporarily stepping outside the rules of femininity, she could maintain an identity as a decent or respectable girl. There are some situations in which the use of aggression is acceptable, even for the good girl.

IN A SETTING THAT IS DEEPLY INFORMED by the culture of the code, investing in a public persona as a good girl or a pretty girl gives girls a special-status position while also creating a special sort of dilemma. Inner-city girls understand the importance of being known as an able fighter. Yet, like Takeya, many girls would rather not be known as a girl who is ready to fight all the time. These girls, much like Danielle, will submit to fighting only after exhausting all other ways out of the situation. Girls with public reputations as fighters will court conflict and are often ready to "throw down" (fight) at the slightest of violations, a bump or a stare, but girls who wish to be seen as good, as many girls do, fight only when they have to—when they have reached the protective limits offered by situational avoidance and relational isolation. The normative order of violence in the neighborhoods in which these girls live makes it hard and potentially dangerous to be a good girl *all the time*—and girls knows this well.

Finally, in contrast to the girl fighter who embraces her identity as an outsider, the good girl consciously works within the boundaries of normative femininity. The good girl is ever aware of the gendered expectations of family, peers, and teachers; unlike girl fighters, she buys into these expectations and submits—as girls who are perceived as good tend to do—to the types of formal and informal social control that constrain her angry or aggressive actions. She understands very well how those girls who violate gendered norms are perceived and treated by others. She works to distance herself from these girls, and in doing so, reproduces the familiar raced and gendered dialectical relationship between the pretty (good) girl and bad (ghetto) girl that tends to pit groups of girls against one another as enemies rather than allies.

CHAPTER 3

"Ain't I a Violent Person?"

UNDERSTANDING GIRL FIGHTERS

> I really know how to fight. So I really would
> beat her up, real bad, and then leave her
> there. That would be the end of that.
>
> —DeLisha, seventeen

I AM ON MY WAY to DeLisha's house on another hot summer day. Staring out the car window, I notice several men hanging out on a stoop near the corner. Graffiti on the wall behind the group reads, "J Block." This letter-block combination is familiar: it makes me think of the stories I have been hearing this summer from men incarcerated in the maximum-security prison outside of the city. I have been visiting the prison, along with a half dozen other university students, for a weekly introductory criminal justice course offered as part of the Inside-Out Prison Exchange Program.[1] Several of my incarcerated classmates have shared stories about growing up in neighborhoods just like DeLisha's. They talk about the blocks they used to live on—29th Street, 34th Street, 46th Street—and the blocks they live on now: A Block, D Block, J Block. J Block, they say, is one of the prison's most chaotic areas. The porous boundaries between the street and the prison are always there, but the connections are not usually so obvious. DeLisha's block stands out to me for this reason.

Seventeen-year-old DeLisha and her young daughter live in a row home with her grandmother, who raised her, her two brothers, and DeLisha's aunt. When I first meet DeLisha, I notice how different her demeanor is from that of girls like Takeya or Danielle. Those girls work to blend in—they do not want to draw the attention of anyone looking to prove a point. DeLisha, on the other hand, seems to seek, even demand attention. She is polite as she invites me and my companion, a young male medical school student who is along for the visit, into her home, but she is not smiling, and her eyes do not drift away from ours—she looks us in the face.[2] DeLisha takes up space.

Like other girls I interviewed, DeLisha sees life as a struggle, and she is determined to come out on top. DeLisha is the sort of young, Black woman who troubles even the most well-intentioned middle-class people, White or Black, when they encounter girls like her behind the counter at a city drugstore or on the commuter train. She has attitude written all over her face. "I've never had anything handed to me on a silver plate, [like] everybody else did, or however else it happened. But I love to struggle," she tells me during the course of our conversation. DeLisha seems to relish confronting her life's daily battles head on—an attitude towards life that she takes literally. Early in our conversation, she states with confidence and without apology that she has always been all about fighting.

"Was this the first time something like this happened to you?" I ask, referring to the wound she received during her fight with a neighborhood girl.

"Yup."

"This was the first fight you got into?" I question.

"First fight with her?" DeLisha asks.

"First fight, in general."

"Oh, no," DeLisha replies with a smile.

"No?" I question.

"Oh, no," she repeats.

"How often did you fight before you got into this fight?" I ask.

"Second grade to the tenth."

"To the tenth?" I probe, hoping for more information.

"My whole—every school I went to was all about me fighting," DeLisha explains. Then, in a way that reinforces her tough demeanor, she continues, "Every school, from elementary, to middle school, to junior high, to high school."

In contrast to girls who are reluctant to fight, and do so only when they feel they *have* to, DeLisha represents herself as committed to a fighting career. Her claim to be all about fighting defies common expectations about girls' behavior: Violence is generally considered femininity's polar opposite. Yet, as much as DeLisha's disclosure challenges what we currently believe to be true about violence and about girls, I found that her tone, demeanor, and perspective were quite typical of a significant segment of the girls I encountered and interviewed. These girls who fight and win regularly, whom I describe as girl fighters, make sense of their struggle to survive in today's inner city by becoming all about fighting.

Girl fighters, like their good girl counterparts, must make choices and take chances as they pursue the intersecting survival and gender projects in today's inner city. This chapter examines these decisions, and the conditions under which they are made, in order to understand how and why a girl like DeLisha becomes a fighter. Why does she invest so deeply in crafting an identity that places her so far outside both mainstream and local expectations of femininity?

This chapter offers a contrast to the experiences of good girls who work to meet the expectations of appropriate femininity that are reflected in the image of the Black lady. Similarities and differences in the beliefs and behaviors of girl fighters, who are more likely to be evaluated by others as ghetto, are revealed when juxtaposed with the life experiences of the good girls described in the previous chapter. Girl fighters craft a somewhat defiant presentation of self that emerges from the isolation, frustration, and anger that poor, Black girls internalize early in their lives. Both good girls and girl fighters are invested in what they think of as the struggle. But the good girl's accomplishment of survival depends more heavily on her investment in a gendered identity that deviates only slightly from mainstream expectations of appropriate femininity and is generally consistent with notions of a respectable Black femininity (Collins 2004). In contrast, girls who craft a fighter persona directly challenge the relatively restrictive and potentially dangerous expectations of appropriate femininity in this setting. A girl's reputation as a fighter may protect her from certain challenges and allows her certain freedoms, while also making her more vulnerable to retaliatory actions that range from non-verbal looks and stares to life-threatening assaults.

The narratives of the teenaged girls I interviewed reveal two common pathways to becoming a fighter. I describe these in the next section. I then critically consider why a girl might embrace an identity that distances her from what is commonly understood as gender-appropriate and respectable behavior. I ground this discussion with an extended narrative that focuses on Terrie, a high school junior who describes herself as a violent person. I conclude the chapter by considering some long-term implications of the ways in which gender works at the intersections of race and class to keep girls in their place. What does the future look like for a young Black girl who visibly challenges such restrictive expectations in her day-to-day life? Do girls like DeLisha forfeit forever any claim to traditional expectations of femininity? Will they always live by the code of the street? Can they ever become something other than a fighter? If so, how?

REAL BOYS, GOOD GIRLS, AND GIRL FIGHTERS

In American society, as in most others, gender lessons begin in early childhood. Boys learn early on that aggression and dominance are fundamental elements of manhood. Family members will directly or indirectly encourage aggressive behavior in boys while discouraging it in girls in ways that make aggression seem natural or essential to being a boy. Girls, meanwhile, are encouraged not to be like boys. They are taught at an early age to restrain their anger and physical aggression.

How, then, do girls like DeLisha craft their reputations as fighters and how do they reconcile the gendered contradictions that emerge when a girl fights like a boy? In many ways, the process of crafting a public persona as a fighter is not unlike what boys do to convince others that they can "go for bad" (Anderson 1999) or that they are "badasses" (Katz 1988); nor is it especially different from what girls like Danielle (see chapter 2) do to convince others that they are good. What good girls and girl fighters have in common is, first, a shared structural-cultural context that is shaped profoundly by entrenched poverty, the threat of violence in everyday life, and by the code of the street. This shared context leads to a preoccupation with survival, including a conscious and active imagining of what to do next in order to ensure personal safety. The intersecting and overlapping aspects of inner-city girls' identities—poor, young, Black, and female—put them in an especially vulnerable position.

Some popular media images and songs reinforce cultural lessons about the value of being a tough, strong, and independent girl.[3] Teenaged girls do hear songs about men who need a woman who is ready to physically battle with others, called a "ride-or-die bitch" in one song, if and when necessary. Such representations of Black women provide a newly defiant image of Black femininity that is rooted in the same type of physicality that characterizes the experience of the young, urban male.

These cultural messages also reinforce the survival lessons that are passed along to young women from family members and peers. At the intersection of these messages and media images, the tough girl who fights and wins emerges as a possible identity. Some teenaged inner-city girls may already sense that being perceived by others as a good girl is somehow beyond them. Their hair may be the wrong texture; their demeanor may be too loud.[4] Since violations of gender expectations such as these frequently result in formal and informal sanctions, girls with these attributes also may have earlier and more frequent opportunities to acquire and hone fighting skills. In this structural-cultural context, the good girls come to believe that their best chance for survival lies in staying close to home and meeting general (and gendered) expectations in school: staying out of trouble is key to survival for these girls. In contrast, girls with reputations as fighters come to rely not on their looks but on what they can do. These girls learn to value agency over passivity and strength over weakness. Because their everyday environment is one saturated with messages about the fragility of personal safety, girl fighters come to take a special sort of pride in their ability to fight and win.

BECOMING A FIGHTER

There are, no doubt, many ways in which girls go about constructing their identities as fighters. Among the girls I interviewed, two routes emerged as most common. The first pathway opens spontaneously, during unsupervised play with other kids in the neighborhood. In this kind of setting, when a girl gets into a fight, the response from her peers is largely unmediated by adults. This makes it possible for a girl to craft an identity that contradicts normative expectations of gender without having to fear serious sanctions from adults, and with the significant benefit of building self-confidence. An elementary school–aged girl who knows how to fight and win gains a special-status position among her peer group, one that enables her to subvert efforts by family members, school personnel, and some peers to shape her behavior in gender-appropriate ways. The second potential pathway to becoming a fighter typically develops later, is more deliberate, and involves the intervention of at least one family member. Because danger is an acknowledged aspect of inner-city life, some families choose to protect young members by passing along defensive skills to both boys and girls. A young girl's male family members may teach her how to fight in response to an actual or a perceived moment of vulnerability.

Each pathway transmits cultural lessons about the importance of strength and toughness. These lessons alone, however, are not enough for a girl to become a fighter. Embracing that identity involves at least three steps: a girl fighter prioritizes individual assertiveness over perceived weakness; learns the necessary skills to make her an able fighter; and is gratified by the feelings associated with fighting and winning. This third aspect is perhaps the most significant of the early gender violations performed by the girl fighter—a good girl does not like hurting other people. In contrast, the girl fighter embraces this feeling, and in doing so, she directly challenges the constraints that other girls seem to submit to more willingly. She comes to believe that she is better than other girls, perhaps especially the good or pretty ones. This sentiment encourages a greater sense of self-confidence, which gives the girl who fights a significant advantage in self-preservation. Adolescence is a time when most girls grow less self-confident and begin to internalize the negative stereotypes associated with women and girls.[5] By the time a girl reaches high school, she is experienced in trading on her carefully crafted front as a tough girl who can box (fight with her hands), a person others should be wary of challenging. High school, however, also introduces a new arena, one that requires girls to reestablish their reputations.

COURTING CONFLICT: LOOKS, BUMPS, STARES, AND "THE FIGHT"

Typically, girls who know how to fight are far more confident in handling potentially aggressive situations than girls who have never fought. Girls do not have to be highly skilled fighters relative to boys. They will stand out as fighters because most girls do not invest time in learning how to fight. Since fights do not happen every day, girls who are truly committed to crafting a fighter identity must court conflict by engaging in strategic "campaigns for respect" (Anderson 1999) in order to create the types of interactions that will reaffirm their position. Here, too, they violate normative expectations of femininity—good girls do not court conflict, they avoid it. A girl fighter courts conflict using the same arsenal of interpersonal micro-assaults her male peers use: looks, stares, and bumps. Being a fighter requires that a girl not only maintain a tough front over an extended period of time, but also that she actually fight when a non-negotiable point of confrontation is reached. Like the badass, she must always be open to challenge and she must never fail any challenge—there is no time off for the girl who has committed herself to becoming a fighter (she must be, as DeLisha says, "all about fighting") (Katz 1988).[6]

The moment of dramatic realization (Goffman 1959)—the fight—is brief, fleeting even, especially relative to all the time and effort invested prior to that moment. Still, it is necessary. For girls, no less than for boys, the fight provides the opportunity to prove one's reputation to a larger network of others. The high school fight is particularly useful in shaping this public persona precisely because most fights are gratifyingly messy and short spectacles. Students, who tend to know how long it will take school security officers to arrive on the scene, will begin to break up a fight before these adult authorities arrive. The evaluation of the fight, its winners and losers, begins as soon as the fight ends. The group of onlookers is transformed into a network of interpreters who collectively ask and answer questions about who won. Without the audience, the fight has no meaning. The collective answer the group reaches has serious consequences. The group's interpretation of a fighter's performance not only determines whether or not a girl retains her status as a fighter, it also can shape what happens next, including whether or not escalation or retaliation is necessary.

THE USES OF AGGRESSION AND VIOLENCE

By the time a girl is known as a fighter, she has embraced an identity that directly contradicts expectations of normative femininity, which bear heavily upon her life. She stands in contrast to general depictions of femininity as well as locally defined notions of respectable Black femininity. She is not passive or submissive. She does not easily defer to power or authority. She is not a good girl in the minds of others. She is an outsider. Such an identity is protective, but at the same time, it can make a fighter more vulnerable to challenges from others who are trying to prove a point as they craft their own fighter identities. Girl fighters are also more vulnerable to sanctions for violating gender expectations. Their distinctly unladylike demeanor is likely to attract negative attention from school officials, for example, with the result that she is likely to receive harsher treatment when a real or imagined violation occurs—it is easier to punish the girl who does not act like a girl.

Thus, being known as a fighter can simultaneously protect a teenaged girl and make her more vulnerable. In order to understand why some girls refuse to just go along with expectations of appropriate feminine behavior, we need to critically consider what benefits might be associated with *not* being a good girl, to understand what she gets from physical fights and her fighter persona in general.

In the most basic sense, the girl who is known as a fighter gets what everyone wants and what most of us spend a good deal of time seeking: an identity (we all long to be somebody) and respect. While the respect of our peer group matters to most of us, in settings governed by the culture of the code, it takes on a critical importance. In settings that are governed by the code, respect that is based on strength and the potential for dominance matters not only to an individual's constantly developing sense of self, but also to her or his struggle for survival. Both young men and young women gain a sense of power or control over their lives when they take their survival into their own hands, figuratively and literally. This sense of power is especially important to those girls whose particular intersection of race, gender, and class make them more vulnerable than others. While the sort of power that is derived from the code is seemingly hypermasculine—based as it is on the coupling of physical strength with social dominance—it is not restricted to men only.[7]

The reality of this power is real and the girl fighter's embrace of it as more than an act is revealed in girls' accounts of why they fight. These explanations often describe the catalyst for the transformation of anger or frustration into action as a desire to put right a perceived injustice that might otherwise be ignored.[8] Sharmaine, an eighth-grader, explains that she uses her strength and power to challenge the gendered hierarchy in which she exists:

"Why were you fighting this time?" I ask.

"Because boys like to think that they can hit on girls, but they can't hit on me."

"So why do you fight boys?"

"Because I don't like to see boys hit girls."

Sharmaine explains that when she sees a boy hit a girl, she calls him on it: "Don't you know that you not supposed to hit no female?" That explicit and public challenge usually "starts something" that Sharmaine is committed to finishing. In this

case, Sharmaine is using her power in a way that both challenges and reaffirms—reconstructs, even—the gendered hierarchy that initially positions her as powerless. She readily calls a
boy out because he is not showing girls proper (gendered)
respect. A boy does not hit a girl, the lesson goes, because girls
are weaker than boys; yet Sharmaine uses her strength—her
physical strength—to challenge this assumption. She also uses
her power to challenge the normalized degradation of girls,
which occurs in the form of "calling you out your name" that
adolescent boys (and girls, too) engage in at school.

"Plus," Sharmaine continues, "the boys at my school
always want to call you out your name."

"Like what?" I ask.

"Like bitch, slut."

"Do they just call you out your name, or other girls too?"

"Like half the girls they do, but I don't like that. It be making me real angry."

It is Sharmaine's final comment that shifts our attention
from what normalizes the use of physical violence—the culture
of the code—to what helps fuel a young girl's commitment to
crafting an outsider identity as powerful and volatile as a fighter:
anger. Black feminist scholars have written about this anger
over the last several decades, and the conditions in which
African American, inner-city girls are coming of age have only
worsened over time. The use of physical aggression or violence
provides a way for girls like Sharmaine and DeLisha to express
their anger, to intervene in the power dynamics that oppress
them, and to try to make things right, on their own. Sharmaine
knows she can fight and win. She can, and therefore she does,
physically intervene in order to avoid becoming either a hapless
victim or a dismissive observer of the budding misogyny
expressed by boys her age.

In some ways, it may look like girls are simply posing or
modeling the behavior of boys and men. Yet, such a cursory

analysis overlooks the serious concerns at the heart of girls' battles, including concerns about respect. Failing to acknowledge the fact that girls too share these concerns about respect and reputation in a context where these things matter minimizes girls' lives. Rather than emerging as a thinking girl, a girl with agency, a girl who is actively trying to make sense of her social world and who she is in it, a girl who is determined to make it, a girl who fights and wins is typically portrayed as incomprehensible, decidedly deviant, or delinquent.[9] But once we acknowledge that girls can and do take some satisfaction in the ability to take care of themselves, to defend themselves, to handle their own business, the next step—seeing girls like DeLisha and Sharmaine as something more than gender mimes—is easy. And that step, in turn, readies us to seriously consider the larger goals that may motivate girl fighters: the desire for space, mobility, and freedom.

The good girl isolates herself from people and situations she considers dangerous, that is, those that pose a threat either to her physical well-being or to the preservation of her self-image as respectable or decent. From the fighter's perspective, the good girl is trapped—imprisoned by traditional and/or local notions of femininity and by a lack of physical skills. Nearly all of street life is off limits to the good girl. Typically, we believe that it is the girl who is out on the street that is labeled as bad *because* she is on the street; however, the girl fighter presents us with a contradictory example. Because the girl fighter has the skills and the willingness to "go for bad" (Katz 1988), she is able and eager to be in the street and to enjoy the freedom that she comes to associate with being in places that others—perhaps especially the good girls—consider dangerous.

For a teenaged girl like Neka, the respect, status, and self-esteem gained from being known as an able fighter provide the necessary freedom and security to pass the time casually on the block, and to walk the hallways of the high school with confidence. Neka, who is in her early teens, often hangs out on the corner in her neighborhood until the late hours of the night. Although fights occasionally break out while she is there, she tells me that she never feels unsafe. Instead, she enjoys herself, relaxing and listening to others talk: "I just be outside . . . like having fun. . . . I just be outside. Everybody be outside and I just be sitting there, like, laughing and listening to them. But they be like bustin' on each other and making jokes and stuff, or they just be talking about stuff." Thanks to past battles fought and won, Neka can occupy more interesting places, including places that are considered male spaces and that are commonly perceived as too dangerous for teenaged girls—places like the corner.

The price paid for this mobility and freedom is that the girl fighter sees herself as constantly involved in a battle. One indication of the intensity of this battle is the frequency with which fights are followed by a quest for retaliation. During interviews, the way girls described the end of a fight often would reveal their plans for payback. Those who were satisfied with a fight's outcome usually closed their stories with something like "that was that," indicating that the fight was over and there was no plan for or expectation of retaliation.

Sometimes, however, payback was planned. When I spoke with DeLisha about the fight in which she had been cut, her demeanor suggested that she judged the outcome of that encounter unsatisfactory. I asked about her plans for the future:

"So, do you think you'll end up in a fight with her again?"
"Yeah."
"You do? Do you think you're going to end up . . . ?"
DeLisha interrupts, "Yeah, it's going to happen."
"Yeah?" I question.
"It's going to happen because I'm not going to let her keep saying what she wants to say to me. I'm not going to let her keep disrespecting me," she states firmly.

I ask DeLisha if there is a way she can avoid another fight with this girl. She replies with an explanation that first highlights how much of her social world is made up of public space:

> We live in the same neighborhood. She lives around the corner from my house. She know the same people [as I do]. . . . She goes to every basketball game. She walks around the neighborhood. People I know, know her. It's just—she works at Dwayne's [a neighborhood take-out], I go to eat at Dwayne's, so it's nothing that we can really stop from seeing each other. She goes to the same market. There's no other market around here, [so] she has to walk up the block. She has to walk past my house to get to the market. She doesn't have to walk past here to go to work. She can go any way to go to work, but she chooses to walk up this block, and she chooses to walk down this block, however way she chooses. But one day she's going to choose, and it's going to be the wrong decision.

Whether they like it or not, these two girls' lives are close. Their worlds are made up of shared public space and overlapping networks of association. The everyday choices they make come with consequences. DeLisha is not interested in investing in patterns of situational avoidance in order to avoid a potential conflict. Doing so would contradict fundamental beliefs she holds regarding her claim to freedom and mobility in her neighborhood:

> I'm not looking over my shoulder for nobody. I walk the streets as though I know where I'm going and how I'm going to get there. Everybody and whatever happens on my way there is going to happen. That's one thing about me. I never be like, well, at a certain time, I'm not going to walk outside, at a certain time I'm not going to do this. No!

If I've got somewhere to go and I need to get home and it's two in the morning, I'm going to go home. If that's where I want to be at two in the morning, or however time it take me to get there, that's where I'm going to go. I'm not a scared type to walk on the street at no time. I walk on the streets anytime I want to. I do anything I want to, anytime I want to do it. It's never been a problem walking on the street three o'clock in the morning. If I want to go home three o'clock in the morning, I'm going to go home. I'm not looking over my shoulder. My grandma never raised me to look over my shoulder. So, I'm not going to start because of a little incident that happened.

DeLisha's assertion that she does and will continue to "do anything I want to, anytime I want to do it" is especially striking given recent events in her immediate area. She lives in a neighborhood that was thrust onto the front pages of the city newspapers and local network news broadcasts when seven dead bodies were found in what was believed to be a crack house, located around the corner from DeLisha's home. This massacre was the largest in the city's history. DeLisha's refusal to allow anyone else to define where she can and cannot go reveals a willingness to take responsibility for her own safety, even in a setting where violence occurs with a troubling regularity. Urban, adolescent girls who have fought and won repeatedly during the course of their adolescent years share DeLisha's fierce desire to freely occupy the space outside their homes. If necessary, these girls will physically fight to maintain this sense of freedom.

Terrie's narrative, which I turn to in the next section, highlights the potential opportunities available to a girl fighter. Terrie's story shows how girl fighters, like good girls, manipulate good and ghetto expectations in navigating the code of the street.

"AIN'T I A VIOLENT PERSON?": TERRIE'S STORY

When we first meet, Terrie, who is just completing her junior year at a local public high school, is dressed in jean shorts and a white tank top. Her hair is neatly tied up under a silk scarf. She stands about five feet eight inches and her well-built frame carries about one hundred and sixty-five pounds. She has a dark-chocolate-colored complexion. Terrie lives in an old row house not far from Philadelphia's university area. The streets that cluster around the university campus form a somewhat integrated neighborhood, populated with working-class Black people and university students. A pedestrian bridge that crosses over a set of regional railroad tracks marks the neighborhood's edge. On the other side of the tracks is Terrie's neighborhood. There, residents—from drug dealers to grandmothers—live in homes that often share a wall with abandoned or condemned houses. During most of the spring and summer months, the interior of Terrie's home is completely dark. Besides shutting out the sun with shades and curtains, the family's only weapon against the summer's heat and humidity is a single box fan. There is no central air-conditioning system, which is considered a necessity in suburban homes outside of the city. The fan sits in the middle of the sparsely decorated front room. The room's other focal point is an eighteen-inch television set that seems to be on all the time.

Terrie lives with her mother; her mother's fiancé, a man with a peaceful presence and a face framed by the long beard favored by Muslim men; and a collection of real and "adopted" sisters. She has not seen her biological father, who is currently serving time in one of the state's prisons, in years. However, the man she refers to as her "real dad," her mother's ex-boyfriend and the one who chose to be her father, remains a stable presence in her life. Terrie's mother, who Terrie considers a best friend, works two jobs and is home just two nights of the week.

Terrie is charged with taking care of her little sisters during the
day. In addition, she plays the role of unofficial counselor on
her block, listening and providing advice to most of the
younger kids in the neighborhood when they come to her with
questions and concerns.

Terrie and I spend most of our time talking on the covered
porch outside her front door. It is here where I first meet Uncle
Slim, another member of Terrie's family. Slim is a rail-thin,
dark-skinned man with a generous but toothless smile. He is, as
I will learn firsthand, also a relentless flirt. Slim wears the same
worn work clothes each time I see him. His worn blue jeans,
worn white T-shirt, and worn construction boots hang loosely
on his lanky body, which is also worn, it seems, by manual
labor and cheap liquor. Slim steps onto the porch and greets
Terrie with a big hello and some good-natured teasing. He
quickly casts his gaze on me.

"Who are you?" he asks.

Terrie intercedes, explaining quickly that I am "a lady"
who is talking with her about violence.

"Oh, violence, huh?" Slim responds.

"That's right," I confirm.

"Oh, I'm violent," he says.

"No you're not," I joke. "You're a softy, I can tell."

Slim's smile disappears. He begins to lift his right leg up,
barely an inch off the floor, as he lowers his right hand into a
small pocket on the side of his pants. He slowly draws his hand
out, briefly revealing the handle of a knife in his leg pocket. As
he continues the motion, he fully exposes the blade of a knife
that was completely hidden just seconds before. Holding the
handle of the knife, Slim stares directly into my eyes. I do not
feel threatened, but I do get his message: if necessary, good-
natured Slim can get down, and fast. Returning his gaze,
I smile and let out a short laugh. He smiles and then releases a
hearty laugh. He announces that he has to head to the corner

store for some cat food and a 40 (a forty-ounce bottle of malt liquor).

After Slim leaves, Terrie continues to introduce me to her neighborhood. Most residents seem to know and interact with one another on a regular basis. As Terrie and I sit talking, two older women and one older man walk by. Terrie acknowledges each person individually, by name (e.g., "Hi, Mrs. Johnson"), and each of her greetings is returned with a "Hi, sweetie." In between greetings, Terrie's detailed report flows on. She covers the occupants—including the children, dogs, and cats—of almost every house on the block. When a young man wearing jeans, a sweatshirt with a white T-shirt that hangs to his mid-thigh, and construction boots walks by, staring into his cupped hands, Terrie comments, "See that boy right there? He's a drug dealer. Look at him with all that money," she directs, as the young man flips through a clip of green bills. Terrie has positive things to say about almost everyone in the neighborhood except the block captain, who has refused to open the fire hydrants on the hottest days of the summer, and the residents of a house around the corner.

According to Terrie, that house is a center for illegal activity, including drug selling and arbitrary violence. Terrie says, "There's a house around the corner, with like sixty kids in it."

"Sixty?" I question skeptically. "No way."

"No, okay, not like sixty. Like at least fifteen to eighteen, and they sell everything there. The grandmom sells platters [of food]. They sell puppies. They sell drugs. And they have kids living there too."

Terrie tells me that one of the boys who lives in the house recently lured a cat down a closed alley. The boy then let his dog, a pit bull, follow the cat. After the pit bull attacked and ultimately devoured the cat, the boy had turned and shouted to the friend for whom he had staged this show, "See, I told you that my dog is on cats!" Terrie says that she later challenged this dog owner, demanding that he either train his dog or keep it off the street.

The Corner Store Boys

The corner at the other end of Terrie's block is where the corner store boys hang out (their name comes from the old storefront that marks the corner). This spot is a center of open-air drug trafficking, and much of the violent activity that occurs in the neighborhood takes place here. While the corner is relatively quiet during the day, by 6:00 P.M. activity picks up as the drug dealers go to work. "Sometimes," Terrie tells me, "the little kids be hustling too." She quickly reels off the names of several people, with varying degrees of commitment to the corner's activities, who have been shot in recent years. Like many others in her neighborhood, Terrie distinguishes between victims whose own actions put them in harm's way and those who were simply in the wrong place at the wrong time. She mourns for one young boy who was shot last year while "just standing there . . . he wasn't even a drug dealer or anything"; she is less sympathetic toward her own cousin. He was shot standing on the same corner but, Terrie explains, rolling her eyes, he is now "back on the corner doing the same thing he was doing," selling drugs.

Recent efforts to curb open-air drug trafficking in the city's neighborhoods have not had any effect where Terrie lives. As she sees it, "Things are getting worse. There's more drug dealing on the block." Terrie bases this conclusion on the number of new faces that have begun to appear on the corner. These people are strangers; she does not know them and has not even seen them before. Terrie is now more careful to keep the younger kids in the neighborhood away from the corner once it gets dark. Doing so may protect them from some of the violence. Nonetheless, because so much legal and illegal activity is organized around the corner, violence can spill uninvited into the lives of everyone in the neighborhood, especially when the block gets hot and police surveillance and enforcement activities increase. The following excerpt from my field notes provides a sense of how such episodes unfold in the neighborhood:

> I drove to Terrie's house today, and when I slowed my car to make a right onto Terrie's block, I was blocked by a police officer standing in the middle of the street, with a police car on either side of him. The corner was full of young men, brown-skinned men, most in white T-shirts and baggy jeans. All of the young men stood around nervously. While none of them were in custody, all were aware that they were under surveillance, and perhaps most importantly, they were aware that they were not free to leave their corner just yet. Young women and men from the block gathered at a safe distance, across the street from the corner. There was little talking between neighbors and a lot of staring at the police officers, the police cars, and then back to the boys on the corner. When the police officer returns to his car, I am able to make a right onto Terrie's block. I notice that neighbors are out of their homes and on their stoops, all eyes on the scene that I have left behind me. I quickly find a parking spot and join Terrie's younger sister and best friend on Terrie's stoop. As I approach the stoop, Terrie's sister, who is as skinny as the iron railing she is dangling on while staring towards the corner, turns her head to smile at me, and then returns her stare to the corner.
>
> "What's going on down there?" I ask, mostly to the back of their heads.
>
> "It's getting hot," Terrie's best friend explains. It is clear that she is not talking about the weather but commenting on the pressure felt by many residents when police activity

in the neighborhood increases. "The cops chased that boy down the alley."

"The boys on the corner?" I ask.

"Mm, hmm." Terrie's best friend, demonstrating the appropriate wariness reserved for people who ask too many questions, simply repeats, "It's getting hot."

When I return to my car moments later, two young boys between the ages of six and seven whiz by on their kid-sized bicycles. A dark-brown-skinned boy in jeans and a T-shirt wears a concerned look on his face.

"My brother got locked down?" he is asking, as if to verify a piece of information given to him by his friend, who trails him by several strides.

"Yeah," his friend responds, breathing a bit more heavily. "Your brother got locked down!" he yells as the two young boys race with childlike urgency to the corner.

When I finally catch up with Terrie, she explains that there had been a shooting around the corner earlier in the day. Because of their ties to the corner, "they [the corner store boys] all became suspects." It is through scenes like this that drug dealing, the various forms of violence associated with it, and the lessons of the code affect the daily lives of neighborhood residents. For younger residents—boys and girls—the local drug market and the related violence are stable features of neighborhood life and the code of the street that governs this aspect of daily life is real. This is the context in which Terrie has developed and sustained her reputation as "a violent person," as she tells it.

They All Know Me

"Everybody around here knows me," Terrie tells me as we sit on her porch. "If you tell them that you know me, you cool. They all know me."

"So," I ask, "if I get into some trouble around the neighborhood, then I can just tell them that I know Terrie and I'll be cool?"

"Yup," Terrie replies confidently, leaning back in her folding chair as she takes in the view of the neighborhood. She is known on the block, and when she walks by the corner, the people hanging out there all say, "Hey, Terrie." "See," she confirms, "they all know me."

Everybody knows Terrie because, after living in the neighborhood for fifteen years, she has built a reputation as a "violent person." Terrie locates the origin of this identity in her very first fight, which took place in this same neighborhood nearly twelve years ago. The fight happened down the block from her house, next to what is now an abandoned lot, when Terrie was six years old. She and her best friend were playing with two boys who were new to the neighborhood. Even at a young age, Terrie was aware of how physical attributes sorted people, hierarchically, into appropriate categories. Terrie had her young heart set on "light-skinned" and "skinny" Michael. Since Terrie was also skinny "back then," she decided that she should play with Michael, and her then chubby friend should play with Michael's friend, "the chubby one." One day, as the four kids were playing, Terrie's plan seemed to be going well. Michael had a pair of roller skates and had offered to let Terrie use them after he was done. Terrie happily accepted his offer, but then her best friend also asked to use the roller skates. Michael, oblivious to Terrie's plan, agreed. Terrie remembers being "so angry" at her girlfriend for disregarding an arrangement that seemed both right and settled to Terrie. Michael was "hers." She channeled her fury into her fists and fought her best friend. In her memory of this first fight, Terrie was the winner. In the twelve years since this event, Terrie has fought repeatedly, and with each victory she has strengthened her reputation as a young woman who can fight. The fights Terrie gets into now are meant to protect that reputation and the authority and respect that enable her to navigate her neighborhood and the public high school she attends.

Most of Terrie's fights, now that she is in her late teens, occur at school. She describes a typical scenario, beginning with the initial, instigating event. One morning at school, one of Terrie's female cousins approaches and informs her that another young woman at the school is "stepping to her." Terrie's cousin is likely to end up in a physical battle with this young woman unless someone intervenes. This is why the cousin comes to Terrie and why Terrie tracks down the adolescent girl who stepped to her cousin. She begins by talking with the girl. According to Terrie, she and this young woman agree to "squash" the potential fight after Terrie explains a simple truth: If the girl steps to Terrie's cousin, she will also have to step to her. At this moment, in Terrie's mind, the argument is settled. It has been ended by the strength of her intervention. However, later in the day, Terrie's cousin reappears, reporting that the young woman has stepped to her again. Terrie recognizes this action as a direct violation of the agreement reached earlier in the day. The fight, Terrie stresses as she recounts the story, was "supposed to be squashed." Therefore, the girl's latest action represents a flagrant sign of disrespect toward Terrie. Essentially, she has called out Terrie and now Terrie must decide how she wants to respond.

Terrie chooses to publicly challenge the girl. She catches up with her in a school hallway. Other young people, who tend to gather quickly at the scene of any potential fight, promptly surround the two. As Terrie turns to say something to a friend, her cousin sees that the young woman challenger has begun preparing for a fight: She has taken off her wig and is wrapping a scarf around her head to prevent the hair-pulling that sometimes happens if a fair fight goes "wild."

"She's about to hit you!" someone warns, calling out from the crowd. Recognizing that she will soon be at a disadvantage if she does not strike first, Terrie turns around and punches the young woman in the face. As additional punches are thrown, the teenaged girl bites down on Terrie's hand. Terrie grabs the young woman's head with her other hand and leverages her own body weight to bang the girl's head into a vending machine. Blood spills from the woman's face and drips into the open wound on Terrie's hand. School security guards finally reach the center of the fight and break it up. Terrie is promptly suspended. She goes home concerned more over how best to deal with her mother's response to the suspension than over what to do about her obviously injured hand. She continues to ignore the gash until this area of her hand has doubled in size as the result of an infection. Terrie finally visits the local hospital emergency room, where her infected wound is cleaned and stitched closed. As she remembers this visit, Terrie rolls her eyes and tells me about a doctor who told her that she "shouldn't be involved in that violence stuff." Terrie is aware of the "non-violence" rhetoric, she tells me. But in her neighborhood and in her school, it is preserving her reputation that matters most in protecting herself.

It's Not All about the Boy

This need to maintain her reputation and the continuing significance of skin color among African American girls underlie a second and more protracted series of aggressive encounters that Terrie describes to me. "Light-skinned" Alisha is a new-comer; she came to Terrie's school earlier in the year. And while other young women warned Terrie that Alisha was a "man eater," a young woman who is not to be trusted around any-one's boyfriend, Terrie extended a welcome anyway. A week later, she had reason to regret her generosity. Alisha had begun flirting with Terrie's not-quite-ex-boyfriend.

The stage for the first confrontation between the two teenaged girls is one of the most public places in the high school: the lunchroom. According to Terrie, Alisha is the initiator. She interrupts a conversation Terrie is having with her ex. Stepping past Terrie, Alisha "put[s] her face all up in his face" and asks to borrow a dollar. To Terrie, this act, played out in front of an audience, constitutes a pivotal point of disrespect and thus requires some form of response. Terrie immediately challenges the young woman because, as she reminds me, "I've got a reputation [to maintain]." After chastising her ex for allowing Alisha to interrupt their conversation, Terrie follows the young woman into the hallway, where she proceeds to make a larger scene than the one Alisha initiated in the lunchroom. As an audience gathers, Terrie explains to Alisha, and to everyone else within earshot, why she is about to beat her up: "*First,* I'm going to smack you for being all up in his face while I'm in there talking to him. *Then,* I'm going to beat you up because you know that was my man."

Terrie's threat complicates our understanding of what it means to fight over a boy. For Terrie, the fight seems to be more about being disrespected than about the potential loss of a boy's affections, although the fact that the source of both the disrespect and the flirting was a light-skinned girl termed a "man eater" likely heightened the intensity of her anger. Before the confrontation can escalate into a physical battle, however, a security guard forces the girls to leave the area and reminds Terrie that if she fights again she will be expelled. Terrie is aware of this constraint, and she was aware of it when she chose to call Alisha on her disrespectful behavior. But, as Terrie said, she has a reputation to protect.

The constraints within which Terrie works as she upholds her reputation as a violent person are significant. She cannot allow the challenge from Alisha to go unmet, but at the same time, she must avoid being expelled from school. The rules, as

Terrie understands them, are simple. If she hits first, she will be expelled. So she does not hit first. Instead, each day, Terrie bumps Alisha while she is walking down the school hallway, hoping that eventually this will provoke Alisha into hitting her. By Terrie's logic, if Alisha hits her first, and all she, Terrie, does is respond—purely in self-defense—she will not be expelled. Alisha, whose reputation is not defined primarily by her fighting ability, never does hit first. The school year ends with her still simply absorbing the blows from an individual who is widely acknowledged as a formidable challenger. Each time Alisha fails to respond, Terrie's reputation is validated.

Trade-offs

If Terrie is, as she is reputed to be, a violent person, why doesn't she just fight Alisha and get expelled? The answer is relatively simple: Terrie's identity as a violent person is not really who she *is* but rather a role she plays, a front that she has developed over time and now uses to facilitate her interaction with others as well as her movement through both her neighborhood and her school. To some, Terrie *is* a "ghetto chick"—a woman who is not interested in or able to meet mainstream or local expectations regarding acceptable femininity. Yet, one would be incorrect to conclude that Terrie is *essentially* a violent person or, in turn, essentially and irreformably "ghetto." Erving Goffman's discussion of the presentation of self in everyday life is helpful in considering the performance Terrie is deeply invested in (1959).[10] Goffman's explanation encourages us to consider Terrie's story not as a story of a violent girl per se, but rather, as a story of how a teenaged girl embedded in the culture of the code may *use* a tough front and, at times, violence to negotiate for safety and respect in her everyday life.

The maintenance of this front does not necessarily require continually engaging in physical fights. For example, Terrie's victorious public and bloody hallway battle with the young woman who challenged her kept her reputation as a violent person intact for most of the school year. In the aftermath of that fight, new stories about Terrie's fighting ability circulated throughout the school. She did not need to publicly reaffirm her reputation until a new member of the school community, Alisha, challenged her with a public display of disrespect. However, since Terrie's reputation as a fighter is so strong and the constraints she is operating within so public—everyone knows that if she fights again she will be expelled—she does not actually have to fight Alisha. Rather, she simply has to make it clear that she is not letting Alisha get away with anything; thus, she repeatedly tests Alisha, and her own reputation, through "bumps" in the hallway.

The ongoing conflict with Alisha does not fully satisfy Terrie's need to continually reaffirm her reputation, however. Occasionally, she sets up other school-based tests. For example, walking down a hallway, Terrie came across two girls, at least juniors, she says, who were standing in a threatening position in front of another girl, who Terrie thought was a freshman. It was clear to Terrie that the two girls were preparing to fight this freshman girl, who had no backup in sight. The unfairness of this situation, she says, struck her as "just not right."

"How are you just going to roll up on someone like that? Two girls and she by herself?" she asks me. Terrie stepped in front of the two girls and asked why they were "messing with [her] little cousin." The duo quickly explained that they were tired of her little cousin's big mouth.

"Well," Terrie retorted, "maybe you have a big mouth." She made it clear that if the two young women had a problem with her little cousin, then they had a problem with her. Apparently not up to this challenge, the girls retreated promptly.

Since this showdown, Terrie's newly minted cousin, acutely aware of the protection she receives from her association with Terrie, has repeatedly thanked Terrie for coming to her aid. She also continues to trade on this association as she makes her own way through the school. Terrie explains that whenever her "cousin" sees her in the crowded halls of the high school, she yells out, "Hey, Terrie!" loud enough for everyone to hear. Terrie laughs as she tells me this. Terrie always says, "Hi" back but, she confides, she "still has no idea what that little girl's name is." Ultimately, the girl's name does not matter. Terrie clearly derives a sense of power and self-confidence from intervening in an unfair situation and making it right simply through the strength of her own reputation. Perhaps most importantly, however, she has tested and validated her reputation once again, and she has managed to do so, once again, without having to fight, thus avoiding expulsion.

After recreating this history of her violent and potentially violent interactions for me, Terrie sits back on her folding chair, looks around, and then announces, "I'm a violent person." She pauses for a second and then says once more, "I'm a violent person." Recognizing that this sort of self-definition is insufficient, Terrie searches for someone to validate her claim. Almost as though on cue, her nine-year-old sister leaps up the crumbling concrete porch steps. "Dana, ain't I a violent person?" Terrie asks. Barely lifting her head, Dana lets out a quick, confirming "Yup" and just as quickly bounds back down the porch steps. Terrie's reputation, although cultivated mainly in the school setting, also helps to maintain her position in the neighborhood as a person of authority, someone "everybody knows." Finally, as Terrie sees it, keeping her reputation as a violent person believable means that she can continue, with little possibility of harassment, to do such atypical things as attend her Advanced Placement classes in chemistry and several other subjects, visit local colleges with other juniors who also have aspirations for higher education, and make plans to enroll in a summer program for gifted students at a local, predominantly White university.

The Future for Girl Fighters: Unmaking Meaning

After listening to their stories, I wondered what the future would look like for girls like Terrie and DeLisha. I did not wonder whether they would continue to struggle—the current conditions of inner-city life virtually guaranteed that they would—but would they always be fighters? The girls' stories suggested that sometimes a specific event or events—personal injury, extreme neighborhood violence, or perhaps a glimpse of a different, better set of life possibilities—would prompt a fighter to reconsider her commitment to this identity. Yet, these reconsiderations appeared to be momentary, and as fragile as they were fleeting. Each girl's movement toward a different self or her hope for a break from the struggle seemed to overlie a deeply rooted fear that to make such a move or to have such a hope was not only impractical but also foolish and, ultimately, dangerous. In order to truly pursue a different path, a girl fighter must disassociate herself from the identity she has so carefully crafted and loosen her commitment to the meaning embedded in the fight.

Teenaged girls who are deeply invested in their fighter identity believe that they are fighting *for* something: status, respect, mobility, or freedom, qualities usually summed up as reputation. Much of their energy is given over to protecting their reputation, which is, both in their minds and in the culture of the code, integral to their struggle for survival. Of course, fighting and maintaining a reputation as a fighter require a great deal of physical and emotional energy; one has to be on and open to challenge all the time. Over time, girls, like their adolescent boy counterparts, can become exhausted by the everyday battles, physical and symbolic, that make up their struggle to survive. For some, this fatigue may prompt an interest in finding an opening, a pathway out of being a fighter. A hint that this fatigue has settled in lies in the meaning that inner-city, adolescent girls attach to their battles.

For some, the fight goes from being about something very important to being "about nothing," in Sharmaine's words. Sharmaine expressed her fatigue after her most recent fight with an adolescent boy. When I asked her what this fight had been about, she told me that it "wasn't really over nothing." In contrast to the stories she told me about earlier fights, which had featured principled justifications for her actions, this fight narrative was empty. Sharmaine's response was not much of a narrative at all: she did not set the stage and she provided no elaborate definition of the situation. The fight was just "about nothing." In contrast, for Neka, fighting is still meaningful. She continues to be deeply embedded in the rhetoric of respect, and the strength of her commitment is not shaken by either the actuality or possibility of injury:

"After [the shooting] happened I didn't really change. It just—I just had a wound on my face. I really didn't . . . I was still like . . . I didn't change, nothing really changed about me."

"Did you think, 'What if it wasn't a BB gun? What if it was something else?'" I ask.

"Nothing," she replies.

"Do you think that maybe some of these fights that you get into with this other young woman could ever end up badly?" I ask.

Neka laughs. "No," she says.

"Do you think anything can happen from it?"

"No. Uh-uh."

"Do you think you can actually lose the fight?" I press.

"No. . . . Nope. Unless somebody try and jump me, but that's not going to happen."

Neka is not wholly ignorant of the potential consequences associated with an ongoing commitment to "the street." She knows that if you get into a fight, "you can get beat up or hospitalized or locked up." She does not think any of these things will necessarily happen to her, however, and she remains hypersensitive to any signs of disrespect. She is still deeply committed to the fight for survival in its most literal sense.

Each time I reviewed Neka's sure response to my question about whether or not she could actually lose a fight, I found myself thinking about my conversation with DeLisha. I could easily imagine DeLisha giving me the same response if I had interviewed her five years earlier. But, as a young mother who has survived her share of real and symbolic challenges, DeLisha's view of the future is not the same as Neka's. Her injury seems to have significantly affected her thinking about her life as a fighter. Usually, DeLisha is on the winning side of fights with other girls: "I was always doing the hurting to somebody," she tells me, reflecting on her history. "I never cut nobody, never poked [stabbed] nobody or nothing. I always fought with my hands. But, this is the first time something ever happened to me. And [she] was the reason I got cut."

When I ask DeLisha if this makes her "feel different about fighting," she says, "Yeah." I ask why.

"It makes you feel like you never know what somebody's going to do because they are scared to fight you or they scared you're going to hurt them. So, you got to think about the odds and ends [when] you're about to fight this person. Are they going to fight me fair or are they going to cut me, or they going to do something to you, to hurt you? So, I've slowed down."

DeLisha's decision to "slow down" has also been influenced by the trauma of a recent mass murder in the area, which has "cooled people out" in the neighborhood, including her. The extreme violence of the massacre, combined with "people just dying everyday, people that we know, family members—all types of stuff," gives DeLisha pause and makes her reconsider the violent interactions that are regularly played out on neighborhood streets: "You don't ever know what people go through in their house. And then to go outside on the street and deal with the street problems too?" It is in this last comment that I hear both DeLisha's desire for a different world and her weathered realism that such a world does not yet exist. This is the dialectic that defines the "struggle" undertaken by young girls who live in neighborhoods like DeLisha's.

What about those girls who eventually leave these neighborhoods behind? What will become of those who manage to manipulate the code of the street in a way that allows them an opportunity to exit? What will girl fighters do in settings where violence is not a normal part of everyday life? Will they change? I cannot answer these questions with any certainty; the girl fighters' futures are no clearer to me than to them. Yet, girls' accounts reveal that context matters. Since much of their fighting behavior emerges from the pernicious circumstances in which they come of age, it easy to imagine that this behavior would lessen in settings that ensured their safety and security. Indeed, there are hints in some girls' narratives that suggest the possibility of compromise and adaptation.

Terrie already suspects that fighting with looks, bumps, stares, or fists is not a part of the "code" at college. She tested this assumption after a recent tour of the campus of a local, predominantly White university. When the tour was over, Terrie asked the guide, in the presence of other prospective students from similarly distressed neighborhoods who were part of the tour group, what would happen if someone was in the cafeteria and spilled Jell-O on someone else "and that person got all hype [instigating a fight]?"

"Oh," the tour guide replied, "everyone would just look at them like they were crazy. People don't do that here. Everyone's grown up."

Of course, as Terrie may one day discover, "everyone" who attends college is not "grown up," but the circumstances of daily life on a university campus, even one located only blocks from her own neighborhood, make it not only possible but mandatory to establish and maintain a comfortable level of personal security without recourse to hands and fists. In making their way in the world outside the inner city, girls like Terrie must step to completely different challenges, beginning with the daunting task of casting off their fighter identities.

CHAPTER 4

"Love Make You Fight
Crazy"

GENDERED VIOLENCE AND
INNER-CITY GIRLS

IT IS 10:30 ON A WEEKDAY MORNING and I am riding the trolley
as it moves along its route underneath Philadelphia's Center
City District. I notice two African American girls in their late
teens sitting across from one another near the door of the trolley car. They are both dressed in black jeans and white shirts—
color combinations that are consistent with the dress code in
Philadelphia's public schools. The girl who is sitting across from
me sports the kind of puffy black coat that has been in style for
months.

In a voice loud enough for other passengers in the car to
hear, she addresses her friend, "I can't believe he choked Justine
like that." Her girlfriend offers no audible reply, but the young
woman continues anyway. "That's what she get," she says,
intuiting that Justine must have done something to instigate the
choking.

This remark elicits a response from her friend: "She
smacked him." The two talk a bit more about what they both
clearly perceive as having been a dumb move on Justine's part.
They do not, however, place all the blame on the victim. "He
too big to be hitting on some little-ass girl. He too big to be
hitting on Justine. She a little girl." As I listen, I am troubled by
the logic underlying the girls' exchange, but not surprised.

Versions of stories like Justine's, including her role in what seems to be her own victimization, surfaced during interviews with young women who participated in my study, often when they were talking about the experiences of some other girl: a friend, a family member, or an associate. Generally, the girls I spoke with about such violence believe there is a set of rules governing teenaged girls' physical conflicts with adolescent boys and men. These rules reflect mainstream expectations of appropriate behavior for boys and girls, and are influenced by—yet are also distinct from—the code of the street. The notion that there are symbolic lines that neither teenaged girls nor women should cross during arguments with their boyfriends or male partners is pervasive. In the different settings I frequented during the three years I spent in the field—the local public school, the city jail, the trolley, neighborhood streets—many of the girls and women I encountered shared this belief. One of the most obvious violations, and one that is likely to produce (deservedly, in some people's opinions) physical retaliation from a man, is a blow to his face. If a teenaged girl hits a young man in the face and he hits her back—well, as the girls on the trolley put it, "That's what she get." At the same time, teenaged girls also have ideas about what men are supposed to do in confrontational situations. In Justine's case, the man who choked her crossed the line not because he hit her—by their logic, she deserved that because she smacked him in the face—but because he was too big to choke her.

The exchange I overheard on the trolley illustrates elements of a common theme regarding teenaged, inner-city girls' understanding of dating violence. First, although it is generally accepted that men should not hit women, some teenaged girls are quick to offer qualifications. These circumstances, to a troubling degree, point to their peers' (or sometimes their own) culpability for such violent encounters: A young woman who hits a man should expect to be hit in return, the logic goes. Many young men and young women empathize with this position. Danielle (introduced in chapter 2), in describing a fight she had with her boyfriend, explained to me that during the fight she became extremely frustrated. Her boyfriend, she said, kept "getting all up in my face." That combined with continuous back and forth yelling finally resulted in Danielle smacking him across the face. Her boyfriend, who normally is a shy and reserved young man, did not hit her back. Aware that she had crossed a line that left her open to the possibility of retaliation, Danielle said she felt lucky that her boyfriend had not struck her. In addition, she explained, this experience made her understand how some young men might hit young women, even though, in her words, they "don't really want to do it." Others, however, like the teenaged girls on the trolley, suggest that even if a young woman is responsible for instigating a physical conflict, this does not entirely absolve a young man who hits back; they know that a hit from a man can do far more damage than a hit from a woman. Thus, in Justine's case, while she may have deserved to be choked, the young man who attacked her should have stopped there.

As I listened to these stories and thought about the relationship expectations they reflect, what I found especially troubling was the uncritical resignation with which these girls accepted the violence that was meted out to other Black women and girls and the readiness with which they blamed girls and women for their own victimization. Of course, this sort of response is not unique to the residents of America's inner cities. Much of life in inner-city neighborhoods reflects the same sort of gendered power dynamics present in mainstream American life. Such beliefs are exacerbated by poverty, not originated in poverty.[1] While many young women in distressed inner-city neighborhoods have stories to tell about what social scientists would define as dating or domestic violence, few girls use that terminology to describe their experiences. Instead, they trade stories about friends or cousins who were hit, gripped up (roughly grabbed), or choked by their boyfriends during an argument. The justifications for this violence are familiar—she asked for it; she deserved it. Yet, the negotiation of intimate abuse in distressed inner-city neighborhoods also includes a unique quality shaped by the circumstances of life in this setting. The most notable of these circumstances is the lack of resources available to help young men take on a masculine identity in ways that do not involve physical domination or violence, and the equally limited resources available to help young women protect themselves from everyday threats of violence in their relationships with boys and men.

In this chapter, I consider how the circumstances of inner-city life shape relationships between young women and men, and in particular, how it contributes to the attitudes toward and responses to aggression and violence in these relationships. How might the code encourage violence against women and girls? What resources are available to the inner-city girl who is negotiating a violent relationship? When and how do inner-city girls fight back? I provide answers to these questions by analyzing several instances of gender-specific violence that were described to me by three young women, Terrie (introduced in chapter 3), Lacy, and Amber. I met with each of these teenagers several times during the study; they revealed their stories to me over the course of our meetings. Their experiences are not intended to be representative of those of all inner-city girls who are negotiating forms of gender-specific violence or abuse. The stories Terrie, Lacy, and Amber tell, however, do illuminate the very complicated relationship among poverty, the culture of the code, and gender-specific violence.

"I DON'T PLAY THAT"

Adolescent girls' exposure and vulnerability to sexual assault and violence in dating relationships vary in degree and consequence. Girls who live in distressed inner-city neighborhoods learn how to respond to these threats in various ways. The spectrum of responses, which includes situational avoidance and relational isolation, ranges from silence to aggressive physical resistance.[2] Girls who have crafted reputations as fighters may believe that they are able to meet physical challenges and may respond physically in a conflict with a relative or an intimate partner. If someone hits them, they hit back. Of course, this tough exterior does not protect girls from every sort of violence that may be directed at them.

Of all the young women I encountered, Terrie, a self-described violent person (see chapter 3), came across as the toughest. Physically, she is at least as big as boys her age. She carries her weight with confidence, and she offers no apology for engaging in the sorts of fights that directly challenge normative expectations of feminine behavior. She is a fighter, and proud of it. Her fighting skills have afforded her a degree of protection from the types of situations encountered by girlfriends. Terrie tells me about some young women she knows who are trapped in relationships with abusive boyfriends. She is particularly worried about one, an eighteen-year-old girl she has not heard from in several days. This girl recently moved in with the forty-year-old father of her newborn. Terrie, who knows this man is abusive, fears for her friend's safety.

As Terrie relates these stories, the mix of worry and disgust in her voice reveals her confidence in her own ability to avoid being forced into a similar situation. She would put up a fight. To illustrate, she recounts a recent argument with her boyfriend Ray. It was one of the hottest days of the summer and Terrie was dressed in what she calls a wife beater, a man's tank-top-style undershirt, and shorts. Ray thought the shirt was too revealing and demanded that she change her clothes. Their argument "got heated" (quickly escalated) and then became physical when Ray "put his hands on" Terrie. Her reaction was immediate and decisive. "He gripped me up . . . but I don't play that. I hit him back and left." In challenging Ray's physical dominance—"I don't play that"—Terrie also challenges the oppressive gendered dynamics that trap her girlfriends in abusive relationships. Terrie resists Ray's attempts to act out his masculinity on her body. First, she hits him back and then, she leaves. These two actions disrupt the gendered power dynamics that are the foundation of many heterosexual relationships, dynamics that can be especially dangerous for couples who live in distressed urban neighborhoods.

While Terrie is adamant that she will never be trapped like her friend, she is also aware that there are certain types of gender-specific threats that she is less capable of avoiding. Her tough front was shaken during a recent visit to a corner store in her new boyfriend's neighborhood. After she stepped into the store and began walking down a short aisle, the male store clerk made his way to the front of the store and locked the door. As Terrie recreates this scene for my benefit, I can see something in her face that I have not seen during our previous conversations: fear. Terrie pauses for a moment and I share her silence, imagining all the terrible things that could have happened to her; sexual assault—rape—is, of course, at the top of that list. I suspect, by the worried look on her face, that this is Terrie's primary imagined horror as well. She continues the story, telling me that after seconds that seemed like an eternity, a customer appeared at the store's glass entrance door. The clerk, startled by the customer's abrupt arrival, unlocked and opened the door, and Terrie slipped out, unharmed.

When Terrie returned to her boyfriend Derrick's house, it took her a few moments to calm down. After she got herself together, she told Derrick what happened and he became furious. In the same way that Ray's response to Terrie's choice of clothing reflected a certain understanding about how real men handle their women, Derrick's response is shaped by the masculinity resources that are most accessible to him within the culture of the code: anger and physical violence. He threatens to go to the store immediately and shoot the clerk. Terrie convinces Derrick not to do so. In recounting her plea, though, she reveals a hole in the protective buffer her tough front typically provides. If she wanted the clerk to be seriously injured—to be shot—she would not need to rely on Derrick. Neither, though, would she need to take action herself. "I have brothers to do that," Terrie says.

Terrie's experience at the corner store exposes the limitations of her carefully constructed tough front. That front does not convey the same sort of meaning to the male store clerk as it does to other teenaged girls in a school setting. To the clerk, Terrie is simply a potential sexual object. Terrie's reputation gives her an edge at school, and her skill as a fighter may be protective in a shoving match with a boyfriend like Ray or Derrick. In the case of sexual assault, however, her ability to define the situation fades quickly, as does her power to fight back. Terrie's relative powerlessness in responding to a potential rapist is further illuminated by her comment that she would call on her *brothers* if she needed to retaliate against the store clerk. This response makes clear the limited set of resources available to inner-city girls who are raped or beaten by boyfriends or strangers. Terrie does not mention even considering calling the police—a decision that reflects her neighborhood's tenuous relationship with law enforcement. Neither does she mention calling a rape crisis hotline, or any other sort of community-based organization. Instead, Terrie relies on those elements of the code that obligate her brothers to defend her honor, along with their own.[3]

It is hard to know for certain what might have happened had the customer not knocked on the storefront door. Would Terrie have been attacked? Would she have been able to fight off the clerk if he did indeed attack her? Would she have told her boyfriend or brothers if she had been raped? Fortunately,

Terrie did not have to confront any of these possibilities, yet many African American inner-city girls must do so. Terrie's experience demonstrates that even the toughest young women may encounter threats that exploit the gender-based power differences between men and women that characterize American life and that are exacerbated by the culture and conditions of the inner city.

"HE WON'T STOP UNTIL YOU HURT HIM"

An often unrealized consequence of the general abdication of institutional responsibility in distressed inner-city neighborhoods is the increased vulnerability of young women and girls to various threats of gender-specific violence. Many men are well aware that not only are young women like Terrie unlikely to tell others about their victimization, but also that often there is no one to tell.[4] The physical and social circumstances of the inner city further constrain girls' management of gender-specific threats. Lacy's narrative demonstrates, in particular, how the close proximity of residents and their low levels of mobility complicate her attempts to deter a neighborhood-based stalker.[5]

Lacy, an African American girl in her late teens, describes herself as a "social person" who is often "goofy," and who likes to "play around" with people. After dropping out of high school, she began trying to earn her high school degree through the Nightlight program. She attended classes regularly at first, but has since stopped. Usually, Lacy dresses in baggy jeans or khakis and long button-up shirts or sports jerseys, which give her thick build a boxy appearance. In the colder months, she covers her jersey or button-up with a brown or blue utility coat. She also sometimes covers her hair, which she often wears in cornrows, with a black wave cap. As she walks down the street, it can be difficult, from a distance, to distinguish her from an anonymous young Black male. Closer up, though, Lacy's

diamondlike stud earrings draw attention away from her clothing to her girlish face. The young men who hang out on the
corner generally leave her alone when she walks around the
neighborhood, although once in a while they say something to
her as she walks by.

When we first meet, Lacy tells me she is concerned about a
prostitution ring that is operating out of her South Philadelphia
neighborhood. Her block, like many others in the area, is a mix
of occupied and unoccupied row homes. The long line of cars
parallel-parked along both sides of the street give the block a
closed-in feel. Changes in activity on the street are hard to miss.

According to Lacy's grandmother, the prostitution ring works
by first getting young women hooked on drugs and then
encouraging them to prostitute themselves to feed their habit
and to pay their pimp. Over time, I learn that Lacy also is dis-
turbed by an ongoing conflict with a young man in her neighborhood. She tells me that she thinks this man, who recently
turned twenty-one, is "slow," in her words, and that he likes
her. Lacy has been managing this man's threatening advances
for the past year. She describes an encounter that occurred several weeks prior to our conversation. On that occasion, he
entered her house and attempted to put his arms around her.
The two struggled, and then Lacy hit him with her head. When
he loosened his grip, she retreated to the kitchen and grabbed a
knife from a drawer. With the knife in hand, she chased the
young man out her front door.

Lacy and I spoke a bit about the different strategies she uses
to protect herself. The context in which she is negotiating this
threat requires a delicate balancing act. She admits that her
anger at this young man, his obsessive attention, and the effects
the situation has on her daily life all influence how she does
respond, or how she might respond in the future. She tells me,
"I'm just trying to like, if I do see him, even though I hate him
so much, that when I do see him, I'm just, *man*, if he say

something to me, I really, I might do something." The "something" Lacy has in mind could lead to her arrest or incarceration. "That's why I don't want to carry nothing [no weapon] on me, because I can't stop myself from doing something," she explains. Instead, she attempts to protect herself from victimization at the hands of a man who is essentially a stalker by using situational avoidance to limit her engagement in regular neighborhood activities. Lacy tries to limit her time and exposure on the block; for example, when others are hanging around outside on the stoop during the nighttime hours, Lacy stays in the house. She explains, "I'm really, like, trying. Like, I know he come like late at night, like outside, so I don't like be sittin' outside [on the stoop], chillin' outside. And I really, like, either go somewhere or don't be on the block. Stay in the house or something like that."

Frustrated by her very limited ability to handle her stalker, Lacy has turned to the police for help. But, she tells me, although the police did respond, they were not able to offer any real help because Lacy only knows this man's street name, "Peanut," and not his full name. The latter, according to the officers, is required in order to obtain a protection order. The failure of this last in a long series of efforts to find a solution has pushed Lacy toward her limit. She is not a violent person, but she now feels that she may have to become so.

"Why do you think he keeps bothering you?" I ask Lacy.

"Because he crazy, crazy," she responds. "I think he wants to get hurt."

"He wants to get hurt?" I question.

"Yeah. He want to get hurt," she repeats.

"What do you mean?" I ask.

"It's like he want people to . . ." Lacy pauses to think for a moment and then continues. "He won't stop until you hurt him. That's probably why. Like, we called the cops, we argued and all that, and then the next thing is like to do something. So, it's like he wait until he get hurt. I'm trying, you know, I really want to move so I won't do nothing. I ain't trying to end up in jail, but I'm telling [you], I'm this close to doing something."

"Right," I say, recalling, "the last time, you said you had to come in here and get a knife."

"Yeah, because he grabbed me and then I hit him with my head, and then he like tried to knee me. Then when he let go, I ran and got the knife, and he ran out."

"But that's not something you want to do again?" I ask.

"No."

Lacy does not want to "do something," as she says. Still, she feels she may be pushed to the point where she will have to. She is also aware that over the past year, she has exhausted other possible lines of action. As she explains, she already restricts her own movement within the neighborhood to reduce the likelihood of a potential run-in with this man. She has already called the cops. She also has argued with her stalker and has even threatened him with a knife. Still, he remains a persistent threat. Lacy finally concludes that the next thing to do is to use violence, because he won't stop until you hurt him. She is very aware of the potential consequences of resolving her conflict through violence. As she explains, "I ain't trying to end up in jail." But what else can she do?

"I'm Hurt, but I Love Him": Amber's Story, Part 1

Poor, Black inner-city girls who are involved with boys and men who use physical violence against them are in a precarious position. Not only are they constrained, to some degree, by expectations of appropriate femininity and respectability (Richie 1996), but they must also negotiate this violence in a setting in which there is little trust between residents and police, whose role in responding to domestic violence incidents has increased over the last several decades. A central effort of the antiviolence movement has been to criminalize violence against women.[6] Yet, poor women and their partners are typically living in spaces that are already hypercriminalized; teenaged girls in abusive relationships often are as isolated from the police as the men who abuse them. They are, as well, likely to have family members or friends who have been incarcerated, and so may be hesitant to send another Black man to jail or prison. Mandatory arrest policies for domestic violence calls might also result in their own arrest and incarceration. Inner-city teenaged girls are also dealing with a complicated set of emotions, desires, and economic concerns. Some, eager to be loved, are deeply invested in creating the happy family of their dreams (Anderson 1999, 1990; Richie 1996). Particularly if they become pregnant, young women may find themselves financially dependent on the young men who bring them love and pain. Thus, like many middle-class women in abusive relationships, inner-city girls may make repeated attempts to work it out rather than call on the police or the courts for help. They turn to legal options only when the level of abuse reaches a tipping point and becomes emotionally or physically unbearable. Even those who seek protection orders may not necessarily want their relationships to end. It is the abuse they long to stop. The use of the system in these situations, then, represents a step in the process of negotiating a violent relationship, rather than marking an endpoint, as many activists who oppose violence against women typically imagine.

During my final year of fieldwork, I followed one teenaged girl's attempt to negotiate a violent relationship with her baby's father. Like other girls, Amber is striving for respectability, despite her circumstances. Yet, Amber's story reveals the complicated and at times contradictory set of emotions, expectations, and material concerns that shape a girl's response to intimate violence. Her story also illustrates how important personal power is to young men *and* young women in settings where access to economic resources is limited. For teenaged inner-city boys, especially those who are committed to the street, power is readily demonstrated through the use of physical force and domination, especially over women and girls.[7] Teenaged girls who are in relationships with these young men must find ways to enhance their own power. Amber's story reveals how a young mother can exploit a young Black man's vulnerability both to ensure her own protection and to regain a sense of personal power.

Amber is a nineteen-year-old mother who has lived in a city-funded home for young mothers for two of the last three years. She is about five feet ten inches tall, has a round face, and a medium-brown-toned complexion. Amber's group home—the only home her two-year-old son Keenan has ever known—sits on the edge of the university area in West Philadelphia. This refuge for young mothers with no other place to go blends in with other residential homes, apartment buildings, and student housing in the area. Amber tells me she was placed in the home after the city's Department of Youth and Family Services (DYFS) brought a case against her mother: "When I had [Keenan] me and my mom had got into a fight and they [DYFS] told me not to go back home." This was not Amber's first fight with her mother—the two have been at odds for as long as Amber can remember—nor was it the first time DYFS had intervened in her life. During our second meeting at her group home, Amber describes the abuse that has characterized her life: "Man," she recalls, "my mom abused my sister, and my sister turning thirty, punched my sister in the eye, gave my sister a black eye, blood shot her eye, blood shot my eye . . . she used to beat us with an extension cord when we was little and stuff." When Amber was younger, school officials contacted DYFS after her sister arrived at school with a black eye.[8]

Amber's father has been in and out of her life since she was a child. Her relationship with her grandmother, with whom she lived prior to coming to the group home, became more tenuous as Amber got older. Some of this tension, Amber says, arose from the crowded living arrangements: "My Grandma son was living there, and he wasn't paying no rent or nothing, but I was paying rent because I worked. I was working and going to school. And he wasn't paying no rent." Amber understood that her grandmother's decision about the rent was tied at least in part to the fact that her uncle was HIV-positive and, at the time he was living with them, was very sick. Still, from Amber's perspective, her uncle's condition did not adequately explain why her grandmother used to "get on me about everything, everything. She ain't care she used to get on me about everything, and when I say everything, she would get on me about *everything*." Although Amber tells me on several occasions that her grandmother is always "really negative" towards her, she also sometimes qualifies that critique. She explains, for example, "It wasn't really her. I love my grandmom. It wasn't really her. I don't know [if] she was scared or what, but don't take it out on me." Her relationship with her grandmother worsened when Amber became a mother herself:

"We used to have a good relationship, but when I got pregnant, she started treating me differently."

"Do you think she was mad at you?" I ask.

"Yup," she replies.

In considering how to discipline her now two-year-old son, Amber takes into account her own experience as a child with what she defines as abusive discipline. She is likely to lightly spank Keenan, but she is careful to respect the boundary between discipline and what she considers abuse: "I'm not like that." Elaborating, she says, "I don't hit Keenan. You see what a smart mouth he got, uh huh. I don't hit him. I might get with him [grab or spank] sometimes, but it ain't like abuse, no."

Maintaining this stance requires Amber to resist pressure from others in the group home to punish Keenan more aggressively: "Yeah, like when I first came here, when Keenan was turning one, you know how they start actin' up when they turn one, and I didn't want to chastise Keenan. Like he still need some chastisin,' but I didn't want to chastise him, and me and this lady, Ms. Lee, she used to work here, she used to always get on me about that . . . 'cause she just wanted me to chastise Keenan and do what was right. But I wasn't trying to hear that because people don't understand. Well, maybe I never took the time to tell her what my mom did to me, or whatever. She didn't really know I really didn't want to do that."

The group home currently houses at least a dozen other young women. It is obviously crowded; girls and babies battle for limited space. Amber has her own room on the top floor of the home. The walls of the room are painted pink. None of the rooms in the house have televisions. Amber has a radio, though, which she says helps her fight the sometimes suffocating and depressing boredom of the home. Without the radio, "I'd just be sittin' in here lookin' at Keenan and these walls, really. It's just, I be miserable. I be really miserable." Amber continues: "First of all, we don't do nothin' in this house, okay. We clean up, basically you clean most of the day. You want to be honest? Like, you got to do your chores—cleanin' up after grown, supposed-to-be-grown women. Think they grown anyway, I mean. And you have a lock on your mouth, and I'm the oldest." Daytime hours are broken up with a variety of required classes and counseling sessions. Amber is required to see a therapist in order to qualify for independent living, a city program that assists young women in the city's dependency stream to make the transition from assisted to independent living. She also goes to CityCorps classes, which teach a marketable trade to young women and men who have dropped out of high school. Amber is training to become an office assistant. She is also required to attend literacy and parenting classes. She explains, "I gotta do all this to get independent living. They tell me if I don't continue to go to therapy they'll close my case because I'm eighteen. They could discharge me, but him [she points to Keenan], they might try to keep him, because I don't have nowhere to go." After having spent nearly two years in the group home, Amber is exhausted by the strain of living with large numbers of women and their children under the constraints of social workers and the city. "They be trying to hold stuff over your head, man. I ain't tryin' to be here. I'm tired of being here. Yeah, I go to therapy and it, they, make me feel a little better, but still, I still be mad. Hm-mm. You don't know how mad I be."

That Amber has nowhere to go is a continual source of anger and frustration for her and is complicated by her relationship with her son's father, Marvin. This man, she tells me, has hit, punched, and choked her in the past. The two met almost three years ago. Before she became pregnant, she and Marvin were "just datin' for a little bit." When I ask, Amber admits that she did not know Marvin very well before she got pregnant.

"No. I knew him for like . . . I got pregnant in the summer time, like in June or July, and I met him, like, um, I want to say like in March. When is Easter?"

"April," I answer.

"I met him in April then," she says.

Since they've been together, Amber has given birth to Keenan, has undergone multiple abortions, and has been involved in a series of physical and emotional struggles with her baby's father. Her first serious physical fight with Marvin occurred about a year after their son was born.

"When was the first time that it got physical like that?" I ask.

"When Keenan was like one," Amber answers. "When Keenan was like one," she repeats. "Because I stayed away with him, because when Keenan was born he [Marvin] was gettin' on my nerves and he was doing stuff, so I told him that I don't believe in him no more, and he told me and the baby to stay out his life. So we was like off and on when Keenan was born. We was off and on when Keenan was born, because he was getting on my nerves." While Amber expects to tolerate some level of physical aggression within an intimate relationship, she also recognizes that there are limits, and that Marvin has exceeded them: "At first he used to just grip me up [grab forcefully with both hands] or something, or throw me somewhere, like that. You know how somebody, like, push you on the bed or something? He like never choked me or punched me. He just [now] started on that. Like most men, like, push you out the way or something. Like he was doing that at first, but now he just . . . he go overboard with it." Examples of Marvin's escalating violence over the last year include choking Amber during an argument and sending her to the hospital for treatment, following an argument during which "he was banging [her] head up to the wall." One fight, which occurred shortly after Thanksgiving, I hear about in detail as we sit together, talking, in her pink-walled room.

"So, how you doing?" I ask as I take a seat at a small desk across from the bed where Amber sits.

"I'm fine," she offers, with a short laugh that suggests otherwise. She adds, "I've been going through a lot."

Amber explains that she recently had the abortion she had been seriously considering for several weeks. It was a hard decision, she tells me, but ultimately her rocky relationship with Marvin and the restrictions of the group home, which prohibit her from having another baby and continuing to live there, outweighed other options. "And then," Amber continues, "um, me and my baby father got in a fight right after Thanksgiving. He punched me in my eye. I have the picture right in that drawer."

Amber reaches into the drawer next to me and pulls out a Polaroid photo that was taken by detectives shortly after this fight. "And there's the detective numbers," Amber points out as I look at the picture in my hand, "but I never followed through with it. I didn't go back to court." I sit in silence, taking in the Polaroid image of her swollen face. She looks at the picture with me for a moment and then attempts to explain away the small smile that appears on her face in the photo: "They made me laugh on that picture. I know you was like, 'You all smiling,' but I was laughing 'cause they was like making me laugh. But . . ." She sighs and returns to her seat on the bed.

"So, what happened?" I ask.

"Why he hit me?"

"Mm-hm."

The fight, she tells me, was prompted by the fact that Amber found Marvin in bed with another woman the day she planned to have her abortion. She and Marvin were arguing about that infidelity on Thanksgiving Day. According to Amber, it was a typical argument—"like we always argue about everything and [then] he turned around and he punched me in my eye." I ask Amber what happened before Marvin punched her.

"Were you just going back and forth . . . ?"

"Yeah."

"Did he say, like, I'm about to hit you?"

"No," Amber says. Explaining, she adds, "He was calling me all kinds of bitches while we was walking down the street. We was walking down the street because he was going to go home because I was at my grandma's house [and] he was going to go home and get changed and come back up there for Thanksgiving dinner. And I was just going to the store for my grandma, and me and him was arguing and he was just calling me all these bitches and stuff, and he hit me. He punched me in my eye and the bus was coming. So the bus was coming like down this way, and we was walking straight, so he punched me in my eye and he got on the bus. Left."

When Marvin got home, he called Amber. "[He] asked me if I was all right and I just hung up on him," she recounts. "He called back that day and my sister and her boyfriend went down there. My sister's boyfriend fought him, and that was it."

Amber did not hear from Marvin for almost two months following that argument. Very recently, he has contacted her again. She describes this latest connection with him: "He told my social worker, Ms. Johnson, the one that was downstairs, he told her that he wanted to see me and [Keenan], or whatever, and, um, she said that's not her job. So it's not her job for him to see me too—just for her [to help] him to see [Keenan]. So she told him to write a letter. So he, um, called me. I told him I don't trust him. Mm-hm. I told him that we need to work on our relationship before we get back together, because me and him argue and fight too much."

I ask Amber how she is thinking about "working on the relationship."

She replies uncertainly: "I don't know—I'm not—I don't know. I love my baby's father, and yeah, I might do, I do want to get back with him. I love him. But, I'm not going to keep going through changes for him. Like, I know how I can be. I know I got a mouth on me, but it ain't that bad for you to hit me. I don't know what I'ma do."

Amber's immediate network is limited; she has few people to turn to for assistance in formulating a course of action. Her friends who live in the group home sometimes advise, "No, don't go back with him." But Amber views these girls' advice as suspect because "their baby father not even in their child's life," as she says. In contrast to these women, Amber's baby's father is very much in her life, which draws her closer to respectable femininity than her peers. Amber admits, however, that she is conflicted about whether or not he should remain there.

"My baby's father he used to always, he got anger problems for real, for real. He do. Like he can turn—he be gettin' mad easily. But, um, me and him, I don't know. I do want to make it work out, but I'm tired of him, though. I'm hurt, but I'm tired of him." Amber promptly corrects this last statement: "I'm hurt, but I love him. That's what I meant to say. I'm hurt, but I love him. I love him."

"My Baby's Father"

By her own account, Amber does not stay with men long, yet she has continually come back to her baby's father. In order to understand why she feels drawn to Marvin, we must appreciate the significance of the "baby's father" or "baby's daddy" relationship. These colloquialisms are now used frequently in popular culture. Usually, the reference is a derogatory one that explicitly or implicitly highlights the promiscuity or lower-class status of poor Black women. This popular usage misses much of the term's meaning, however. The biological connection forms the foundation for a set of economic and emotional expectations that young mothers have for the biological fathers of their children. A young woman who is still in a relationship with her baby's father assumes an increased level of commitment from this man, beyond financial support. Such expectations often contrast sharply with those of the baby's father. Elijah Anderson describes this mismatch as the difference between "the dream" and "the game": "[Inner-city] girls dream of being carried off by a Prince Charming who will love them, provide for them, and give them a family. The boys often desire sex without commitment or babies without responsibility for them" (1990, 113). A young man may want a girl to have his baby because of the status fatherhood brings him among his peers. A teenaged girl, however, typically is concerned with having a baby *with* someone, which presumes a different sort of relationship than is typically realized by teenaged parents.[9] For a teenaged mother, increased status can be derived from her baby's father's level of commitment to his child. For example, Amber locates a degree of heightened status for herself in the fact that her baby's father is present in her and her son's life—even if his presence does bring unwanted consequences or "drama," in Amber's words. As she says of other young women in the group home, the fathers of their babies are "not even in their life." Amber is not like *them*. Marvin's presence in Amber's life also provides her with a known, if unreliable, source of affection.

Amber's perceptions and interpretations of Marvin's actions are always contingent on the biological fact that, from her perspective, she has a baby *with* Marvin. As she sees it, once made, this connection is difficult to break. Even if the relationship is troubled, it takes far less energy to negotiate a known relationship than to initiate a new one. Amber reasons that if she is going to be involved with someone, it may as well be the person she already has a child with: "I meet other people, I just go back to my baby's father because, man, look they [men] be sending you through drama, and I ain't got no child with you. You tryin' send me through drama, I might as well go with somebody I got a child with if there's going to be drama. I just really, like, I just think I'll always go back to him. I do love him. I'm not trying to justify what he did, like take up for what he did."

Typically, a baby's father is expected to provide financially for his child. In Marvin's case, his ability to provide for his son rests on his profits from drug selling. Involvement in drug dealing, which typically requires a deep commitment to the hypermasculine ethic embedded in the code of the street, can seriously affect relationships. Amber thinks Marvin's dealing gives him an inflated sense of self, which complicates his intimate relationships. A conversation Amber and I had about how Marvin earns money highlights how Amber understands Marvin's "work," his sense of self, and how he treats her.

"What's he do?" I ask.

"What he do?" Amber echoes.

"Mm-hm."

"He was working at a gas station. He got fired because he was selling drugs there. So, now he's just sellin.'"

"[Does he sell] little stuff or is he really deep into it?" I probe.

"Crack," she replies.

I continue to ask Amber about how Marvin's occupation is related to how he acts towards her.

"His attitude," she replies emphatically and then continues, "You know how niggas get money and they don't know how to act."

"Mm-hm," I murmur. "So you think that that has a part of it . . ."

"Mm-hm," Amber confirms.

"So," I speculate, "if he was broke, he'd be acting different?"

"Mm-hm. His parents done even said that," Amber offers. "My dad even said that. 'Cause I remember when my dad dropped me off at his house, right, and my dad was like, 'See all that money he got in his pocket? Marvin doing something illegal.' Which I already knew. But my dad didn't know. He be like, 'He doing something illegal and his whole attitude is going to change.' And Mom and Dad was right. When guys do that kind of stuff they don't really have no, um, they be thinkin' that they the shit, and they ain't shit."

Marvin "ain't shit," but he is still Amber's baby's father, and she is still connected to him. This link gives her an elevated status position—a sense of being better than similarly situated women in the group home. At the same time, Amber is frequently frustrated by her relationship with her baby's father, and specifically, by Marvin's ongoing involvement with other women. This behavior, which she considers cheating despite Marvin's protestations, is the catalyst for many of the fights between them. Amber illustrates this point as she begins to recount how an earlier fight, which led her to the emergency room, began. Aware that the exact details are now hazy in her memory, Amber nevertheless says with some confidence that "it was probably about him cheating, because that's how mostly all our arguments start off, about him cheating." She asks, rhetorically, "How you gonna sit here and tell me you love me but you steady cheatin'?"

I ask Amber whether she and Marvin were "supposed to be exclusive?" "Like," I elaborate, "did ya'll talk about that?" "About what?" she questions.

I try to explain what I mean by "exclusive." "Like," I start, "you told him that you don't want him seeing anyone else."

"Yeah," Amber replies. However, she also suggests that a conversation like that is not necessary if you are in a relationship with a man you have a child with: "You not supposed to [cheat] if you supposed to be in a relationship trying to make it work. We got a child together and you still actin' out. I ain't tryin' . . . ," Amber trails off in frustration.

In addition to not acting like he is in a relationship with someone he has a child with, Marvin also fails to provide the emotional support Amber desires and expects from a partner. This failure was especially apparent during their conversations about whether or not Amber would have an abortion.

You can't stay [in the group home] with two kids, and I was going to keep the baby. I was going to keep it, but I was un-decidable. And like, but I would ask him what he feel, or how he feel about it [and he] talkin' some, "It's up to you." He always say it's up to me. He never actually sat down like I wanted him to and talk to me. He always telling me that there's nothing to talk about because it's my decision. But there's a lot to talk about, because you know I'm living in a place where . . . you should be tryin' to sit down with me and tell me, like I know my options and he know my options, but if he want me to keep the baby like he said he do, then he would be like trying to show me how we going to make it work, but he didn't do that. He didn't do it. He just kept saying it was up to me, that's it. He just kept on saying that it was up to me.

Young mothers in positions like Amber's must continually take their baby's father into consideration as they weigh their options and make important life decisions.[10] The baby's father may be completely removed from a young woman's life or, as in Danielle's case, fully involved in it (see chapter 2), or the baby's father, like Marvin, may vacillate, moving between those two positions, depending on the circumstances. For a young mother in need of emotional support, financial support, or both, the complex and often highly charged connection to her baby's father can seriously complicate her efforts to end an abusive relationship.

Waiting on Change

During my conversations with Amber, it became clear that her primary concern was not to end her violent relationship with Marvin. What she wanted was an end to his extreme abuse. She could tolerate being gripped up but his punches and choking crossed the line. Amber's reluctance to end her relationship with her baby's father means that she must consider ways to negotiate the conflict and potential threat of violence that comes along with her commitment to Marvin. She would like him to "get his act together," she tells me. Her own experience with therapy in the group home leads her to briefly consider the possibility that couples therapy might produce a change in Marvin. Amber explains, "'Cause like I told him, we can go to therapy, but I don't know how to get like, um, like really get involved with that stuff . . . like I don't know how to go to counseling with your partner." She is not convinced, though, that this option will be what works. Amber admits, "I'm still holdin' on to something that ain't, like, you know . . . like, I think I'm holdin' on to something that's not going to work out because me and him argue and fight too much. That's why I said we need to work it out. Maybe counseling would help, who knows. Some people go back to counseling for a little bit and they turn back to their old selves. I don't know." When I ask Amber if she would get back with Marvin even if he doesn't go to therapy, she says she would, but she adds a proviso: "He got to show me he really did change."

While Amber waits for Marvin to change, she utilizes other strategies to manage the relationship. One of her primary concerns is keeping herself safe from Marvin's assaults. When I ask her, "How safe do you feel generally?" Amber responds,

> Oh, safe, 'cause I don't go around him. As long as I don't go around him, I'm safe. I feel safe here. Yeah, I feel safe here. I feel safe everywhere I go; as long as I don't be around him, I'm safe. That's why I ain't going over his house. 'Cause he wanted me to come see him yesterday and I said no. That's why I made plans with [another man], because he wanted me to come see him and I wanted to be with somebody to get my mind off of him. . . . I ain't playin.' I told him I was scared. He gonna laugh like it's funny when I told him I was scared to come over there. He gonna laugh and say well, ain't nobody thinking about me. Yeah, you're not thinking about me until another argument come up, and then you thinking about me.

Amber uses several strategies, including situational avoidance, to physically avoid her baby's father's assaults. First, she tries to limit her time alone with Marvin in his house. She also tries to distract and distance herself from him by starting new relationships with other men. "There ain't nothing to do here [in the group home]. You be havin' so much to think about, because you can't go out, you can't be around people you like, you only got a certain amount of time on the phone. You have so much to think about, you know what I'm sayin' even though you be doin' stuff, you still got things to think about. It's not like a normal day if you were living by yourself on your own. So, it's being around somebody I like that is taking my mind off of my baby's father for real, for real."

"Hopefully" is Amber's answer when I ask if she ever imagines herself being with someone other than Marvin. Almost in the same breath, however, she acknowledges that if her past is any indication of her future, she's in trouble. "Oh, god," she sighs, "I been with the worst of people." Amber then tells me that she is currently seeing a man twenty years her senior.

"Thirty-nine?" I question, well aware that I am not hiding my surprise. "Where'd you meet him?" Amber laughs as I continue in a tone reserved for light scolding, "Where'd you meet a thirty-nine-year-old, grown man?"

"I act older; he act younger," she says, looking down at her feet as she answers. Then, looking up, she continues in a firm tone, "He don't act old. He don't . . . ," she trails off.

"Where'd you meet him?" I ask again.

Amber's description of how she met her new friend—namely, the same way she "meet everybody else . . . walkin' the street"—reveals how exposed young women in the inner city are. "When you go out and they [men] stop to talk to you," a relationship can begin, she explains. The man's age, Amber insists, is not a problem because, "he don't look old. He nice, dress young. He cute—I wouldn't just mess with no any old body."

Amber's attempts to distract herself by spending time with another man sometimes backfire. That, in turn, indirectly reinforces her inclination to remain involved with her baby's father. For example, after her new suitor cancelled a date, Amber grew enormously frustrated. She had scheduled the date in a deliberate attempt to get out of the house and to stop herself from constantly thinking about Marvin. Her new friend's failure to meet her expectation of the role he would play in her life left Amber angry and disappointed. "I was just sittin' in the house, just thinkin' because I didn't want to be in the house and I didn't want to be around my baby's father. I was just thinking about stuff . . . [I was] mad too." Such disappointments make Amber less willing to rely on relationships with other men to distract her from her relationship with Marvin. When I ask if she sees any other options out there for her besides staying connected to her baby's father or pursuing a relationship with this thirty-nine-year-old man, she replies, "Yeah. Really, it should be about myself getting myself together for real, for real. But, it's like I need somebody to make me keep my mind off of my baby's father for some crazy reason."

Over the three years of her relationship with Marvin, Amber has rarely used the full force of the criminal justice system to protect herself from his violence. She has called the police, but she does not tend to show up for court dates. Occasionally, she will let other men such as her sister's boyfriend handle Marvin in a man-on-man fight. Unlike Amber, these men are able to produce an effect proportional to the abuse Marvin directs at her. The ongoing management of the relationship with her baby's father is, Amber admits, exhausting. She is unsure what it will take to bring it to an end:

It's so tiring . . . you know what, my mom, my mom beat me up on several occasions and I still went back home when I had [Keenan]. That was a wake-up call. Then I didn't go back home no more after that you know. I lived with my grandma, then I came here. I didn't go back home, though. No, because my mom beat me up when I was pregnant with him. I was in the hospital and I didn't go back after that. So, people can talk to you. People can try and talk some sense into you . . . but it, you not going to change until you want to—until that wake-up call hit.

So far, the wake-up call regarding her relationship with Marvin hasn't come. Until it does, Amber is unlikely to abandon her current strategies to manage her unpredictably violent relationship. The wake-up call she awaits can take many different forms, and it can be externally motivated, internally motivated, or both. For example, being severely beaten or being unable to prevent the beating of one's children may serve as the wake-up call for some young women, while for others, like Amber, it may be the profound exhaustion brought on by the long accumulation of physical abuse and unmet expectations.

"SOMETIMES PEOPLE NEED HELP": AMBER'S STORY, PART 2

Amber's two-year stay in the group home never transitioned into independent living. When she finally left, she had no certified job skills and no income other than the $516 monthly payment she received from welfare. She also had no place to live, and so she and her son moved in with her mother and stepfather, sharing their two-bedroom apartment on a relatively quiet city block in North Philadelphia. The quiet of the block is sustained in part by the presence of several abandoned buildings, each marked with the familiar city-issued, orange "condemned" signs. A large, stone Baptist church sits on a corner across from Amber's new home and another church occupies the opposite corner. The building that contains Amber's apartment is divided into three floors of apartments. "It's quiet around here, especially at night," Amber tells me after greeting me at the door of the building. She and I walk up two flights of stairs to reach her mother's apartment.

The neatly furnished two-bedroom unit Amber ushers me into, I learn shortly, accommodates not only her and her son, and her mother and stepfather, but also Marvin. Since Amber's departure from the group home, he has come to the apartment occasionally to spend the night with her. This visit will mark my first experience witnessing Amber's interaction with her baby's father. When we sit down in the small living room, I ask Amber how she's doing and she says, "Fine." She looks as if she has gained at least ten pounds since leaving the group home weeks ago. Keenan, who is nearly three, also has grown, mostly up, stretching his vanilla-cream-colored baby fat rolls into a smooth thinness. Amber says she is happy to be out of the group home and reports that she is looking for a job. While we talk, her stepfather comes out of the bathroom and says hello before going to a back room. Amber is sitting across from me, looking nervously, it seems, in the direction of the second bedroom. I don't know who or what is in the bedroom, and I am unsure why Amber appears uneasy. I ask, almost in a whisper, if it is okay for us to talk. "Yeah," she assures me. We continue to talk for a few more minutes, but she remains distracted.

Then I think to ask about Marvin: "And what about your boyfriend?" At the same moment, the door of the second bedroom opens and Amber's eyes dart in that direction. A young, light-skinned man with braided hair, dressed in an extra-large white T-shirt over loose-fitting gym shorts, steps into the living room.

"Here he is," she says.

"Oh, this is him?" I respond, neutrally. As he makes his way through the living room, Marvin doesn't look at Amber or at me. Amber introduces me anyway. I reach out my hand and he extends his only long enough to give me a weak shake. He barely stops before continuing to a front room beyond the kitchen.

As Amber and I continue to talk, she holds Keenan on her lap, planting kisses on his cheek. He seems comfortable and leaves his mother's embrace only for periodic trips to the front room to bring me a toy. Amber tells me that she cannot read very well and thinks that she needs to take a literacy class before enrolling in a GED program. The GED classes cost $398 and she does not want to waste her money. As we talk, Marvin periodically walks back and forth from the front room to the bedroom. Every time he walks into the room, Amber tightens up and stares at him, as if trying to predict his next move. The tension and potential for violence that she confronts in her relationship with Marvin is tangible.

I quickly wrap up our discussion and after Marvin walks into the bedroom and shuts the door behind him, Amber motions to me that we should go downstairs.

"Okay," I say, "do you want to walk me down?" Once downstairs, Amber confides that she only recently got back with Marvin.

"We got into another fight," she says, holding out her left arm for my inspection.

"What happened?" I ask, staring at the three scars on her arm.

"I got another court date, too," she continues.

"Are you going to go this time?" I ask.

"Yeah, I'm going to go. I told him, too. Because next time, if I don't go, next time when I call for help they [the police] probably not going to help me." She continues, "We just don't get along. We fight about everything . . . ," she trails off and then starts up again, "I just recently had an abortion."

"But you just had one in January, right?"

"November," she corrects me. "And then I just had one in June. That's one of the things that we were fighting about."

"Did he want you to have it, or not have it?" I ask.

"He didn't say anything either way. He said he wasn't going to pay for it, though. So, yeah, he did this to me," Amber says, pointing to her arm, "and I had scratches all over my neck."

Sex and Power

Many of Marvin and Amber's fights are fueled by Marvin's failure to meet Amber's expectations of what a baby's father is supposed to do and not do. For example, they fight over his cheating, which, in Amber's view, is not acceptable when you have a child *with* someone. Another sore point is Marvin's lack of steady financial support for his son. Amber is well aware of Marvin's financial situation. She knows that he has two sources of income and thus would be capable of providing for his son, if he wanted to. Fights also tend to escalate after Marvin has failed, according to Amber, to provide the appropriate level of emotional support. What Amber should do about being pregnant with Marvin's child often lies at the center of these arguments. For example, the fight that resulted in Amber's scarred arm (described above) began when she told Marvin that she was once again pregnant with his baby. Marvin's response to this information was to ask Amber if she was "really pregnant." Interpreting this as a derogatory reference to the games some young women play with baby daddies, Amber retorted that she didn't "live like the other hos you know." This exchange sparked a violent fight and another court date.

Neither Amber nor Marvin seems to want another child together. Why, then, does Amber continue to get pregnant? Part of the answer is contextual and situational. Sexual interaction is, like every other social interaction, negotiated. For Amber, as for many other young women, this negotiation takes place within a context of power. I once asked Amber if she used any form of birth control or protection while she and Marvin were having sex. Her answer highlights the significance of power in sexual interaction. Amber said she had tried Depo-Provera, an injected contraceptive. One shot usually lasts for several months. However, Amber did not return to the clinic to receive additional shots after the initial three-month period because she found the drug's side effects overwhelming. "I bled too much," she told me (heavy bleeding is a known side effect of Depo-Provera).[11] Recently, Amber has taken the pill (oral contraceptive), but she has stopped that too. Again, she was bothered by the side effects, which included weight gain. However, Amber considered her own use of protection against pregnancy irrelevant because, she told me, Marvin had promised that he would "pull out," as she describes it, prior to ejaculation. He did not. Amber assumed that she had an agreement with Marvin, a man she admittedly wanted back. She reminded him of this agreement while they were having sex. He ignored her expectation, possibly because from the beginning he had not been serious about his promise. Amber was left with little recourse when it became apparent Marvin did not intend to meet her expectation. The eventual consequence of this failed negotiation, along with a decreased sense of power and control on Amber's part, was another pregnancy. From Amber's perspective, Marvin *got* her pregnant. "But," she tells me, "I'm going to get him back."

Amber's failed negotiation with Marvin reveals a gendered power differential that, according to Amber, makes her violent relationship with Marvin different from other types of interpersonal conflicts. Amber offers a critical reflection on the similarities and differences between the various forms of interpersonal violence that she has experienced. For example, she admits getting into fights with other girls while she was growing up, but "it was nothing like your own . . . somebody older than you and got more power than you, hurtin' you. 'Cause my mom, she got more power over me than a child my age do." "Right," I agree as she continues, "My baby's father, he a man, so he got more power over me." Amber must figure out ways to correct this power differential as she attempts to manage her violent relationship with Marvin. One of her few options is to use the limited resources of the criminal justice system.

"I Don't Want Nobody to Be in Jail"

Amber is unable to offer a proportionate physical response to Marvin's chokes or punches. When necessary to ensure her immediate physical protection, she or someone near her will call the police. Sometimes, when the police become involved, Amber agrees to press charges. This does not guarantee that she will show up at a court hearing, however. In the time that elapses between a given incident and court proceedings, many abused women change their minds about pressing charges. During this time, young men like Marvin may work themselves back into the lives of young women like Amber, deliberately offering a great deal of attention and affection, in an effort to prevent the women from appearing in court. Once the court date arrives and the case is dismissed because the plaintiff did not show up, such men typically return to their old ways.

Amber and Marvin's relationship fits this pattern. After Amber shows me the picture of her swollen face, I ask her if, this time, she is planning to show up at court.

"If you had to go to court over this thing [Marvin punching her in the eye], would you go?"

"I didn't go," Amber says.

"For this thing?" I ask again, pointing to the picture.

"No, I didn't go," she repeats. "My friend went, but I didn't go, because he would have got locked up."

After the hearing, Marvin told Amber what would have happened had she been there. "He told me what the judge said. He said if I would have went to show up to court, he would have went to jail that day. The judge," Amber explains, "said that he don't want to see him in his courtroom no more, and if he hit me or threaten me, he'll go to jail." Amber admits that she "be feelin' bad" about not showing up. She also explains her conflicted feelings about using the full force of the criminal justice system to manage her relationship with Marvin: "I be so mad at the time, but then I don't want nobody to be in jail. I be honest. I wouldn't want someone putting me in jail."

Amber resists showing up in court until her relationship with Marvin reaches a level that is both emotionally and physically unbearable. Their most recent fight marks a tipping point. She intends to go to court for at least two reasons. First, she is aware that if she does not, she may jeopardize her ability to call on the police for protection in the future. Secondly, she is spurred by a recent deterioration in Marvin's attitude. Since the last court date, he has again worked his way back into Amber's life. However, once there, according to Amber, he has done little. She reports that Marvin does not go to work; he just stays in the house and smokes weed. When he called her the previous day, she asked why he had not returned her earlier phone call. Marvin was, Amber tells me, rude in his response. When she told him "to be nice to her," he said he didn't have to be nice, and, Amber says, he "kept getting smart" with her throughout the conversation. Marvin also has cheated on Amber, again. "We broke up," she announces. She is well aware that his current behavior, which includes calling her and asking to be taken back, is an attempt to get her not to show up for the court hearing. Both she and Marvin also realize that this court case is more serious than the previous ones because when Marvin was arrested, he had a "big bag of drugs" in his socks. Amber tells me that the drugs were not "bagged up" (i.e., ready for distribution). Still, it was a big bag, she says.

Day in Court

The court date arrives, and this time Amber does show up. A few weeks before the hearing, she asks me to accompany her. I agree. The Criminal Justice Center, where Amber's case is scheduled to be heard, is kitty-corner from City Hall in Philadelphia's Center City. As I walk through the building's shiny glass doors, I become immersed in a sea of activity. Long lines wind out from two stations, each fitted with a metal detector and security belt, positioned on both sides of a large hallway. The mix of faces I see around me all look brown, albeit in various shades. After making my way through the security line, I follow the hallway to a set of elevators, join a crowd of other people, and eventually arrive at the floor with the courtroom where Marvin's case will be heard. The hallway I walk down is lined with wooden benches on either side and punctuated every few yards with large pillars that extend from the floor to the ceiling. I can barely see Amber, who has positioned herself and her son behind a pillar. She looks as if she is trying not to be seen. After I greet her, she tells me she is hiding from Marvin.

I settle into the small section behind the pillar where Amber is seated. I quickly begin to feel as if I too am hiding. Court hearings require great patience. The process is long and involves open-ended—and unexplained—periods of waiting, usually in the crowded hallways outside the courtrooms. This is another reason why some inner-city residents are reluctant to show up after a charge has been made. It can seem much easier to handle it yourself. Amber, Keenan, and I sit for an hour before she is finally called into the courtroom for the first time. During our waiting period I become aware of the unabashed gazes others direct at Amber, a teenaged mother in court. I imagine that to these strangers, Amber represents countless young and seemingly irresponsible Black mothers. When, after an hour of waiting patiently, her son becomes restless, a line of potential jurors, who arrived only recently, watch as Amber tries to rein Keenan in. "Sit down," she orders firmly as he bounces out of her grasp and lets out a protesting whine. The two go back and forth in this way several times, shattering the silence in the hallway, before Keenan finally gives in. Meanwhile, several of the potential jurors are casting disapproving glances at Amber. An older

Black woman looks down her nose at Amber, who is now seated with Keenan next to her, and rolls her eyes back as she shakes her head from side to side—her evaluation of Amber as less than respectable is obvious. In a short while more, Amber is called into the courtroom. I remain outside with Keenan. "I want my Amber," Keenan yells after Amber has been inside for only a few moments. "I want my Amber!" Amber's trip to court proves successful. The judge orders Marvin to attend anger management classes and puts him on probation. If he does not attend the classes regularly, or if he violates any other terms of his probation, he will go to jail. Amber tells me that she is pleased with this outcome.

Feeling Powerful

Amber's day in court might seem like a natural point for her to end her involvement with Marvin, but that is not what happens. Rather, the hearing merely marks a stage in the process of negotiating a violent relationship with her baby's father. One thing Amber gains from showing up for the hearing is a sense of protection from Marvin's abuse. The terms of his probation include a restraining order that prohibits his either contacting or coming near her. The outcome of the court case also gives Amber access to power that previously had not been present in the relationship, and this emboldens her. She uses this power, as she says, to "get back" at Marvin. Occasionally she will call him early in the morning, when she knows he is expecting a call from his probation officer. This, Amber knows, makes Marvin angry. Other times, she calls to release her own anger at the situation he has put her in.

"I feel better when I call and curse him out," she tells me.

"But," I interrupt, "when he gets angry, he hits you."

Amber agrees, but she draws a sense of security from the fact that Marvin is legally constrained from hitting her by the protection order. Still, she has already given some thought to what she will do if Marvin does hit her: she will call his probation officer and Marvin will go to jail. "He don't like being locked up," she tells me.

Amber is frank in her admission that it feels good to exercise some power over Marvin, but she is also honest about another reason why she calls him periodically. She wants to get back with her baby's father. "That's what I want," she tells me as she explains a call she recently made. "I called him to get back with him." I point out that since she filed for a protection order against Marvin, she should not be contacting him. She knows that, she tells me. Still, she calls.

Still Her Baby's Father

While the restraining order requires that she and Marvin not have any contact, again we see the importance of the baby's father link. When Amber is low on money, as she often is, she must contact Marvin. If Marvin wants to see his son, he must contact Amber. An additional link that keeps the two connected is that Amber is still pregnant and Marvin is, again, the biological father. Her pregnancy brings back memories of her lack of power and failed negotiations during sex with Marvin. "I'm so stupid," she mutters as, frustrated and confused, she attempts to figure out what to do. Her frustration and uncertainty arise from at least two sources. First, she is concerned about her own physical health. If she were to have an abortion, it would be her third of the year. She has not yet recovered from the havoc wreaked on her body by the two previous procedures. She has gained weight, and she has experienced bleeding and cramping. Each abortion also has left her emotionally drained. Amber has heard stories about the dangers of multiple abortions in one year. She thinks, though, that if she truly were at risk of any long-term injury, the doctors would know that and would inform her. They do have her records, she points out, and "they should take care of me."

The second source of Amber's frustrated hesitation over another abortion is her precarious financial situation. While some part of her holds onto "the dream," she simply cannot afford to have the baby.

Amber and I review her finances over a fast-food lunch after a visit to Planned Parenthood. Each month Amber receives $516 from welfare. She would receive more if she also claimed Keenan, but she does not because "they hassle you when they give you cash." So, instead, Amber splits the small sum of money with her son. Stretching the money to cover three, she knows, would be nearly impossible. At the same time, coming up with the money to pay for the abortion is not easy. Marvin now claims that he will help cover the costs, but Amber is unconvinced. He has a poor record of helping in any way with the son he does have, Amber notes, so why should she believe that he will help her to pay for this? Amber has considered other ways of extracting money from Marvin. For example, she is aware that she could have his wages garnished, but she has not exercised that option. Finally, she is sensitive to the implications of being pregnant "up in somebody's house." "It's ignorant," she tells me.

When Amber does attempt to survive financially on her own, her efforts only increase her frustration and sense of isolation. For example, after several weeks of trying to find a place to live, she calls me, in near tears, to report that she is "still up in somebody's house," pregnant, and feeling quite alone. It is clear that Amber feels like a failure. Amber's desires for a traditional, two-parent, family fit with the expectations embedded in images of Black respectability. Amber holds herself accountable to these expectations, as do others. Yet, on this day, it is clear her efforts to meet these expectations are failing miserably. She is especially distressed at her inability to provide a home for her son, which she imagines as a mother's worst failing.

"My baby doesn't even know where his home is. He keeps saying that he wants to go home, he's been saying that ever since we left the group house," she tells me. Finally giving in to her tears, Amber sobs, "He doesn't even know where his house is."

Marvin has not provided any financial support in the last several weeks and Amber has refused to let him see Keenan unless he gives her some money first. She knows he has the money because he is currently working at a cheese-steak stand, making $300 a week. He is also still selling drugs. So Amber is convinced that Marvin is capable of providing some money, at least for his son. Nearing the end of her first trimester, she feels the pressure to make a decision about whether or not she will have another abortion. I ask Amber what she wants most. Almost immediately, she replies, "I want to be happy. I don't want to struggle."

Amber returns to strategizing about what she is going to do about her pregnancy. "Let me ask you a question," she says. "If I decide to have this baby, are there places out there that will help me, you know, get stuff for the baby?" I tell Amber that I don't know that kind of information offhand. My reply shifts Amber's frustration back to her baby's father: "I hate him. I'm really tired. He doesn't know. I'm so mad. He don't care. I ask him what I should do and he says he doesn't care. Some guys say that and mean you know, whatever you do, I'll be there for you. But he, he just don't care."

"But what if he did care?" I ask, trying to help Amber consider how her relationship with Marvin might end up. "You would marry him?"

"Yes," Amber tells me, she would marry Marvin.

"Why?" I ask bluntly.

Amber's response highlights once again how the intersecting forces of the baby's father link and limited economic resources shape her understanding of Marvin as a decent partner, in spite of the abuse that has characterized their relationship.

"Don't no one else want me, especially not if I have two kids."

"You don't know that," I counter.

Amber responds, "I explain that to my mom [too] but she already had three kids by the time she got married, but she was probably nice and stuff. I'm not nice."

"Yes, you are!" I insist, reaffirming a respectability framework that Amber feels is slipping away.

Amber ignores my attempts at reassurance. She tells me that she'll give me a call after she talks to the members of CHOOSE, an anti-abortion group she thinks may help her secure housing.

The Struggle Continues

After much consideration, Amber has the abortion. The cumulative physical and emotional consequences of her relationship with Marvin, including his abuse and failure to provide any emotional support, lead her to realize after a long three years that "he don't care about me." After the procedure, Amber admits, "I'm glad I didn't keep the baby." This hard choice is now behind her, but the challenges keep coming. She will have to take her baby's father into account for many years to come. Her degree of involvement with him is tied in many ways to her own financial situation. Amber is committed, at the moment, to doing well without Marvin's assistance. She tells me, "I need to do this on my own." The price of independence, however, is not simply high, but seemingly literally beyond her means. Amber sometimes has difficulty making her way through the bureaucracy of the city institutions designed to help people secure housing. Ready money is also an issue. She tells me that an efficiency apartment in South Philadelphia that she inquired about requires an initial payment of $1,100, just to move in. Amber's status as a single mother further complicates her quest for housing because landlords seem reluctant to rent to a single woman with children. "It's hard trying to find a place to stay and have kids," she tells me. Her experience living in a group home makes her resistant to living in a shelter. Amber is frustrated by how difficult it is for someone like her to get help when she needs it. Although she has been looking, she still has not been able to find a job. When she submitted an application at a local drug store, they told her that it would take at least three to four months to respond to her application. She began filling out a job application form at the City Fun Factory (a party supply company) but was put off by the form's request for a work history. "They want a work history, but I don't have a work history. They want a school history. Did you complete high school? No. So, forget them." Amber has considered dancing at a local strip club, as some of her friends have done, in order to make ends meet. "It seem like nobody want to help nobody, unless you like on drugs or something." Amber says, "Sometimes people need help."

AMBER'S ONGOING STRUGGLE, even after distancing herself from an abusive boyfriend, exposes a false assumption that is encouraged by much of mainstream dating and domestic violence discourse, namely that an abusive partner is the central problem a woman faces when confronting gender-specific violence. For Amber, Marvin is but one of the many challenges she faces in her everyday life. In her relationship with Marvin, her overriding concern is with ending the violence, not with ending her connection with her baby's father. She uses various strategies to "manage" Marvin, including situational avoidance. For example, she knows that the likelihood of his hitting her is reduced if she neither lives with him nor completely on her own. So despite her unhappiness over living with her mother, she did so because her stepfather's presence helped protect her from Marvin's violent outbursts. Recently, she has left the apartment and moved in with her son's godmother. Amber is careful not to let Marvin know where she is now living. She is confident, however, that even if he were to find out, the likelihood of her being hit is reduced by the fact that she is living with a group of women. If he were to try something, Amber says, "they would beat him up." Amber must manage this violent relationship with her baby's father while also managing expectations of appropriate Black femininity; she is ever aware that she might be evaluated as less than respectable because her child's father is not in her life and that puts pressure on her to maintain her relationship with Marvin despite the regular occurrence of aggression and violence.

Amber must also manage this relationship in a confusing context where a complicated relationship exists between law enforcement and residents. Inner-city girls who see some allegiance to young Black men may be reluctant, as Amber was, to participate in a process that results in the incarceration of yet another young Black man. Amber is reluctant to use the full strength of the system until the third time Marvin seriously hurt her. By then, it had become clear to her that she had very little power to protect herself from Marvin's abuse and that if she did not appear at the hearing, she would lose her only remaining protection, the power of the police, who she thought would be less likely to respond to future calls if she once again failed to show up in court. In Amber's mind, activating the full strength of the system restructured the power dynamic of her relationship with her baby's father. She gained some power and control and, to a certain degree, this felt good. Her control was, of course, fragile, and it was compromised by Amber's desire for Marvin to live up to her expectations of him as a supportive partner and father—expectations that are somewhat unrealistic given Marvin's commitment to the street. Only after an accumulation of physical abuse and emotional disappointments did Amber realize that Marvin would never become the ideal man she envisioned. Amber chose to have a third abortion and now she is on her own. She has given up her attempts to make a family with Marvin. As she puts it, now it's just "me and my baby."

The experiences of Terrie, Lacy, and Amber, along with the adolescent girls riding the trolley, reveal how the structural, cultural, and social circumstances of the inner city, especially Black gender ideologies that reflect widely held expectations of appropriate behavior for men and women, complicate adolescent, inner-city girls' experiences with gender-specific violence. To identify and understand those complications requires a close inspection of how adolescent girls negotiate threats of gender-specific violence in their everyday lives. Terrie's story highlights the limits of a tough front for girls who feel confident in their ability to fight and win—these girls may not be the typical victims we imagine but they too are vulnerable to sexual assault. Lacy's story demonstrates how an inner-city girl comes to believe that the use of violence may be a necessary last resort in order to protect herself from a neighborhood-based stalker. Her story also highlights the potential consequences, including incarceration, of trying to handle a stalker on one's own. Among other things, Amber's story reveals the complicated power dynamics at play in girls' relationships with their baby's father. Her story also reveals the challenges of relying on law enforcement as the main response to gender-specific violence in distressed inner-city neighborhoods. Eventually, girls may use the criminal justice system to negotiate violence in their relationships; however, for many girls, activating the criminal justice system is not an end in itself. Rather, it is a tool to be used in a multistage process of protecting oneself from an immediate threat of abuse. Once a young woman feels "safe"—that is, once she is somehow insulated from the immediate threat—she may use other resources, including situational avoidance, to manage a violent relationship. Attempts to invert the power dynamic that characterizes an abusive relationship, even when such attempts are only marginally successful, allow some young women to regain a sense of power and control in a setting where they often feel as though they have very little of either.

Conclusion

THE OTHER SIDE OF THE CRISIS

MRS. CARTER IS A MIDDLE-AGED MOTHER whose teenaged son, a burly young high school football player, was in a fight in his public Philadelphia high school. Her son's troubles, however, are dwarfed by those of his teenaged sister, who recently gave birth to a baby boy. Mrs. Carter is especially concerned with getting her daughter to realize that mothers "have certain responsibilities." She tells her daughter that "being a mother is doing what you got to do," which often requires some sacrifice. Mrs. Carter recalls the sacrifices she made for her own children. "I've had all types of jobs," she tells me. "I've been called out of my name [verbally disrespected] many times," she says as she recounts some of her struggles to maintain her dignity at work. She encountered racism when she worked at Philadelphia's naval base, and as a McDonald's employee, she "had people cuss me out. Retail sales. Telemarketing. People get mad, cuss you out." Now that her children are almost grown, Mrs. Carter is "going back to school for medical billing," she says. She is looking forward to a job that involves little or no face-to-face interaction with others. "Now, I'll be done with people," she tells me. "I'll be behind the curtain."

Mrs. Carter's desire to be "behind the curtain," to retreat to the back regions of social life, represents a local knowledge about her own vulnerability in public settings and in certain interpersonal interactions. Her disclosure also reveals that using the strategy of situational avoidance is likely to extend beyond the adolescent years for poor, urban Black women. Her wish for a sort of protective invisibility is one shared by many Black women who have spent years fighting for the most fundamental sort of social respect. Black women who, like Mrs. Carter, spend their working lives in service jobs often are vulnerable to strangers' casual surveillance, inappropriate criticisms, and unregulated anger. Mrs. Carter tells her daughter that this disrespect for Black women in general will make the life of a young Black mother that much harder. "I told her she's Black and a woman, you got it double."

For women like Mrs. Carter, the accumulated investment in developing effective situated survival strategies to navigate the "double burden" or "triple oppression"[1] of urban life eventually comes to resemble a larger, seemingly all encompassing survival project that includes battles at work, home, school, and in the neighborhood. This project can be exhausting for many women: "I'm tired," Mrs. Carter tells me near the end of our talk. "I'm out . . . I'm out of words." "I'm tired" is a mantra recited by many mothers who, like Mrs. Carter, are facing old and new challenges as they try to make their own lives, and raise their children and grandchildren. What Mrs. Carter hopes to pass on to her daughter is a lesson that is familiar to the many women—mothers, grandmothers, aunties, and othermothers— who are trying to raise teenaged girls in troubled and sometimes violent inner-city neighborhoods: urban, adolescent girls must understand that they will face unique challenges not only because they live in the inner city, but also because they must function in a world that is often harder for Black people in general and for poor, Black women in particular.[2]

BLACK FEMININITY, STRENGTH, AND SURVIVAL

Historically, the material circumstances of poor, Black women's lives have required a commitment to raising girls to become strong women who can withstand the sorts of challenges imagined by Mrs. Carter. The narratives of the teenaged girls in this book reflect these locally held beliefs about the value of women's "strength," which has been a "historical force of female power" for Black women (Collins 2004, 193–199). This embrace and expression of female strength, which sometimes contrasts sharply with traditional conceptions of White, middle-class femininity and Black respectability, were considered necessary for Black women's survival and for the survival of the Black community as a whole.[3] African American inner-city girls who live in distressed and isolated neighborhoods or attend racially segregated schools may not fully appreciate the multiple oppressions they are likely to face once they transition from girlhood to womanhood; however, they and their caretakers are quite familiar with the immediate challenges, burdens, and dilemmas that accompany coming of age in today's inner city. In contrast to the relatively privileged lives of many suburban adolescents, inner-city girls, their parents, and caretakers must make complicated choices about safety and survival at very early ages.[4] In many ways, the teenaged girls featured in this book are no less concerned with survival than were strong Black women and girls in earlier periods. However, in today's inner city, where poverty is deeply entrenched, and the culture of the code organizes much of social life, what a girl believes she has to do to survive has changed.

In distressed inner-city neighborhoods, adolescent girls must actively work to develop ways to manage the various forms of violence that they may encounter in their everyday lives, ranging from interpersonal battles at school, to fights with their baby's father or intimate partners, threats of sexual assault, and the unpredictable violence associated with the drug trade. Like their male peers, many adolescent girls recognize that reputation, respect, and retaliation—the three R's of the code of the street—organize their social world. Teenaged girls like DeLisha, Danielle, and Shante appreciate the importance of maintaining a tough front and of demonstrating nerve in social interactions. They accept as a fact of life that "sometimes you got to fight."[5] For these girls, adolescent fears of violating traditional expectations regarding what it means to be feminine are at times trumped by concerns for personal safety and survival.

The stories of girls in this book also reveal a deep concern with survival projects that specifically reflect their class, race, and physical position within the inner city.[6] The use of aggression and violence by young women in the inner city is sometimes modulated by girls' desires to meet expectations of appropriate femininity—perceptions that are deeply racialized. For example, a teenaged girl's desire to become a particular *type* of girl or woman—a good or pretty girl, for example, instead of a girl whom others evaluate as ghetto—can influence the degree to which she willingly takes part in physical battles. Girls' attempts to reconcile the gendered dilemmas that emerge from these situated survival projects sometimes reflect and sometimes resist traditional, dominant views of femininity and locally based expectations of Black feminine respectability.

Inner-city girls are cognizant of the code of the street as a system of accountability in the same way they understand gender expectations. African American, inner-city girls must reconcile the dilemmas and contradictions they encounter while navigating potentially dangerous settings. Girls like Takeya and Danielle, for example, are committed to behaving in ways that others evaluate as good, yet they also come to believe that they must present a tough demeanor and be ready to fight, if necessary. At the same time, these girls will rely heavily on strategies of situational avoidance or relational isolation to minimize their involvement in potential interpersonal battles. Girls with reputations as fighters work the code of the street in ways that directly and often deliberately challenge both traditional and local expectations regarding femininity. Girl fighters may have realized early on that the value placed on their particular set of physical attributes may grant them a status as an outsider, and they may use this identity as a resource to challenge the relational and geographical restrictions that good girls often place on themselves. Some girls may embrace the identity of a "ghetto chick"—for example, she may be ready to fight "all the time"—in order to ensure freedom, mobility, and protection in a setting where she knows that her safety is never guaranteed.

In developing survival strategies that work for them, these girls embrace, challenge, reinforce, reflect, and contradict elements of mainstream and local masculinity *and* femininity. Their adolescent lives are characterized by this *fluidity* between and within the competing and controlling expectations of good and ghetto. The accounts provided by Terrie, a self-disclosed violent person, and Danielle, a self-disclosed punk, and girls like them, reveal that African American teenaged girls coming of age in distressed urban areas are engaged in a racialized, classed, and gendered form of code-switching (Anderson 1999). From this negotiation of overlapping and, at times, contradictory survival and gender projects emerges new forms of femininity that encourage and even allow girls to use physical aggression when appropriate without sacrificing any and all claims to a respectable feminine identity. Learning when and how to move back and forth between good *and* ghetto is essential to their struggle for survival in the most troubled inner-city neighborhoods.

The structural and cultural context of inner-city life, including the rules and expectations embedded in the code of the street, exacerbates the problem of intimate violence in the lives of inner-city girls. Young men with few resources to enact mainstream notions of masculinity outside of their intimate relations find broad cultural acceptance for keeping the young women in their lives subservient with force, if necessary. Amber's story illustrates how the desire to be loved and to make a family outweighs her concern for ending a violent relationship. Her story also illuminates the pressing challenges facing young mothers who possess little social and economic resources beyond what is provided by their baby's father. Girls like Amber, who live each day at the intersection of multiple oppressions, are also likely to feel a deep sense of powerlessness after extended periods of abuse and manipulation. Amber eventually exhausted herself in her attempts to manage her violent relationship with Marvin. She did not gain a sense of power until she was able to use the resources of the criminal justice system, which stands ready to police and punish poor, Black men, to keep Marvin in *his* place. Amber's embrace of a power that is rooted in dominance continues a cycle of dominance and intimate violence that is likely to further marginalize Marvin from mainstream society and increase Amber's vulnerability to Marvin's abuse.

Ultimately, it is clear that strength remains a source of power for teenaged girls coming of age in poor, Black inner-city neighborhoods; however, it does so with a contradictory twist since using aggression or violence to demonstrate one's strength can seriously undermine the collective well-being of a community. Generally, the teenaged girls in this book did not (yet) couple strength with dominance. To the extent that they are representative, this offers some hope that structural and cultural interventions can reduce the increasing numbers of girls who enter hospitals or correctional facilities as a result of interpersonal violence. Without such interventions, the experience of inner-city girls may eventually become indistinguishable from those of their male counterparts, who live and all too often die by the code of the street.

THE OTHER SIDE OF THE CRISIS

Neither the wisdom that I gained from listening closely to the stories of the girls I met nor the methodological approach I used in this study provides an ideal basis for formulating broad policy recommendations. Still, my research does establish the necessity and the urgency of directing the attention of both scholars and policymakers to what I describe as the other side of the crisis. To be sure, poor, young, urban, Black men face a difficult time in America; however, many of the experiences that shape their lives shape the lives of women and girls, too. The survival stories of young, Black girls in urban areas reveal their strength and wisdom, but also their particular vulnerabilities. In order to fully appreciate their struggles, and the strategies girls use to overcome these challenges, we must resist attempts to frame these girls exclusively in the context of sexual deviancy, delinquency, or criminology. This type of approach sweeps away the dignity, humanity, and importance of girls' and women's lives. It is essential that feminist scholars, particularly Black feminist scholars, resist allowing studies of teenaged mothers or gang girls, which are largely grounded in the sociology of deviance and/or criminology literatures, to stand in for the lives of all poor, Black women and girls.[7] The lives of urban, adolescent girls are heavily influenced by the violence of gang life and the drug trade, which are deeply entrenched in the neighborhoods in which they live; however, most teenaged girls in inner-city settings are not gang girls or delinquents. This distinction is subtle yet significant in understanding how urban, adolescent girls navigate inner-city life.

Joyce Ladner noted the danger of this skewed perspective over thirty-five years ago, in *Tomorrow's Tomorrow: The Black Woman* ([1971] 1995), her now classic study of girls in a St. Louis housing project. Her warning has gone largely unheeded. Today, the sociological and criminological literature continues to pay little attention to young Black women's experience with conflict and interpersonal violence, except in the context of their *participation* in criminalized, deviant, or delinquent activities. Those few contemporary studies that do examine the experiences of everyday girls growing up in urban areas tend to find that violence deeply informs the lives of boys and girls, and that gender plays an important role in shaping adolescents' experience with violence.

This book contributes to this developing literature on African American, inner-city girls' experiences with violence outside of purely criminalized or delinquent contexts. Placing young Black women and girls at the center of more research projects in urban sociology would also help to correct what is ultimately a dangerously misinformed and potentially dehumanizing academic tendency to talk about race *primarily* through studies of crime, delinquency, or deviance. This book extends Ladner's tradition of inquiry by starting with a basic assumption that inner-city young women and girls are normal, albeit poorer, and thus more vulnerable than their middle-class counterparts. To be sure, the circumstances of life for the girls whose stories are featured in this book differ greatly from those of the girls described in *Tomorrow's Tomorrow*. Poor, Black girls today are coming of age under economic and social conditions that are far harsher than those experienced by past generations.[8] We have much to learn from their struggle for survival in these settings.

As I talked with and listened to young inner-city residents, I saw the heavy burden they carry reflected in their eyes and in the way they carried themselves. I heard it in their voices. Why is it that inner-city girls must struggle so hard simply to survive? What can we do to make everyday life easier? When I asked my respondents what help they thought they needed, they responded with pleas that highlight how structural circumstances shape their experiences. These young people saw clearly that the violence in their lives was related, in some way, to their own economic and social isolation. The recent national catastrophe of Hurricane Katrina dramatically revealed the need for serious domestic policy to reduce the economic isolation of the nation's poorest citizens from mainstream American life and opportunities. There is a serious need for occupational opportunities in the inner city that provide steady work. A job is more than a pay-check; it is also critical to the development of one's sense of self-worth and connection to the rest of the world. Industry has effectively abandoned a population of workers of color in many large cities across the country. We are in need of national and local efforts that bring work back to these areas and to the lives of these inner-city residents who are struggling not only to survive but also to maintain their sense of dignity.

The existence of decent work opportunities and improved housing conditions would likely influence the culture of inner-city neighborhoods in a way that could reduce the lethal violence that currently characterizes much of inner-city life. Such opportunities would make the easy money image of the drug trade less appealing to the young people who are recruited into the game every year. Their involvement in low-level drug traf-ficking assures the fact that many of these young men, and increasingly girls and women, will have contacts with the juve-nile or criminal justice system, which will further isolate them from mainstream work and positive life opportunities.

In addition to providing attractive alternatives for inner-city adolescents who might otherwise be recruited to sell drugs, we must end the war on drugs, which is effectively a war on young Black men and, increasingly women. I believe that with the wisdom of hindsight, more than one scholar will conclude that the tough-on-crime drug laws of the late-twentieth cen-tury were uncivilized and crudely veiled versions of the Black Codes that sold Black men, women, and children into the con-vict lease system in the early part of the twentieth century. This war with no winners has snared great numbers of young people, channeled them into secure detention facilities, jails, and pris-ons, and then spit them back into the most distressed urban neighborhoods in the country. This cycling into and out of the harsh culture of dominance and violence that exists behind prison walls has disrupted and damaged family and social networks, and has endangered the lives of all inner-city residents. In addition to reducing the likelihood that neighborhood street corners will become battle grounds, ending the war on drugs might also improve the culture of city police departments and encourage police officers to interact with residents of hyper-criminalized neighborhoods in a way that ensures that all city residents—regardless of income status or skin color—receive the protection that they are entitled to from institutions like the criminal justice system.

The structural changes outlined above would improve the everyday experiences and life chances of the inner-city girls and women that I interviewed and encountered during my three years of field research in Philadelphia. These changes would likely have broad, positive effects on both men and women. Yet, there are also certain changes within the politics and perspectives of the Black community—across lines of class—that must occur in order to reduce the burden of the struggle for poor, Black girls today. First, Black leaders who highlight and politicize the crisis of the young, Black male must give *equal* and *simultaneous* attention to the struggles of young, Black girls. We must focus our attention on these girls now. Scholarly and political work must expand to encompass the other side of the crisis—the dismal life chances of poor, urban, Black girls. Ignoring the plight of these young residents of the inner city wastes time, energy, and resources while simultaneously reinforcing the sort of gender politics that have isolated Black women in the past, to the detriment of the entire Black community.

The lack of respect accorded to young Black women—from media representations of "video hos" to everyday interpersonal interactions in which Black girls are "called out their name"—is a fundamental problem that must be central to any discussion about the crisis facing young people of color today. Mainstream representations of the Black female body, which urban girls and boys begin absorbing at very young ages, suggest that Black women are objects, available for White and Black men to use in whatever ways they choose. Each time I share my research findings with other Black women—from academic colleagues to my own hair stylists, who work in neighborhoods similar to those described here—they respond with stories of their own about young, Black girls who have been severely abused, sometimes with at least one immediate family member's knowledge. With every new story, my own frustration over what is allowed to happen to Black girls in general, and to poor, Black girls in particular, soars. These girls are made more vulnerable because of their race, age, and economic status. It is time that mainstream Black leaders—especially men—confront these issues with the outrage, conviction, and intolerance that the violation of Black women and girls demands.

There is one more aspect of the other side of the crisis that must be acknowledged, namely the skin-color hierarchy that continues to inform not only White Americans' perceptions of Black women and girls, but also Black people's perceptions about good and bad Black women. Colorism, notably the privileging of light skin and other related characteristics, has lingered since the end of slavery and continues to permeate girls' sense of self-worth in a way that divides them from one another.[9] Colorism is one of the most dehumanizing and divisive elements of contemporary Black life and it limits the quality of relationships among adolescent, Black girls.

I have found hope and comfort in the strength, perseverance, and wisdom evident among the poor, young, Black women and girls who shared their stories with me. At the same time, I feel a deep sense of frustration and even fear for these girls. Many are so deeply committed to a belief system that they think is protective, but that I know is also potentially destructive. The survivor mentality characteristic of many girls reflects a disturbing sense of individualism that diverges from Black women's experiences in earlier periods—a lack of interest in a collective survival and an almost obsessive concern with one's own survival. This mentality reflects and reproduces divisive racialized gender dynamics. It encourages young women to trust no one. Such a perspective, especially if it is developed early in life, has the potential to shape girls' relationships into early adulthood and beyond.

I also feel an anger that I know is familiar to these girls, and to other Black women across the country, regardless of their class position or the shade of their skin. Despite all of the advances made over the last century, survival remains a struggle for many Black women in America, but especially for poor, Black inner-city girls. Life will continue to be a struggle for these girls until we come together and fight back with the lessons learned from their stories. If I have learned anything from my years of researching and writing this book, it is that the battle for respect, dignity, and positive life chances is not one these girls should have to fight on their own.

APPENDIX: A REFLECTION ON FIELD RESEARCH AND THE POLITICS OF REPRESENTATION

"THINGS ARE NOT GOING TO CHANGE," Tracey says firmly from the front seat of Stephanie's emerald green Honda Civic sedan. Tracey is only twenty-two, but her sense of maturity makes her seem older. She has made similar pronouncements during the three years I have known her, but this time she is exhausted and unusually emphatic, and both emotions come through clearly in this proclamation. Stephanie, who until recently was Tracey's boss, but is now just her friend, counters, as she has done many times before, "But Nikki can represent it to them in their language." Almost immediately, Tracey releases a short puff of air through her lips, rolls her eyes upward, and turns toward the window on her right. In the past, I have freely inserted myself into this familiar exchange. Today, I listen intently, but in silence. I do not want to wake Tracey's two-year-old daughter, who has fallen asleep on my shoulder. I am also tired. As we pull up to the university, where Stephanie is going to drop me off before delivering Tracey and her daughter to their West Philadelphia home, Tracey reaches a decision. "I'm out," she says, relinquishing her part in a struggle that she no longer considers her own: "Ya'll will have me end up fighting, and they'd [the project directors] be like, 'Look, I told you we was right.'" Tracey makes this final declaration as she, Stephanie, and I are on our way back from a shared lunch at a chain restaurant several miles away from the inner-city neighborhoods where we had spent so many hours together, meeting with young people who had been shot, stabbed, or injured, either during a fight in school or on the block. We had visited young people in their homes and spent time together at activities sponsored by the hospital-based violence intervention and reduction project (VRP) that served as my entrée into the lives of the adolescent girls and boys in this book.

Memories of one of those sponsored activities, a picnic, float back. Quite clearly, I recall watching a teenaged boy who sat quietly, trying, failing, and trying once again to make a bandage meant to cover a fresh knife wound stick to his skin. The wound was his reward for backing up his brother during a neighborhood fight. After observing the young man's futile efforts, I sought out a fresh bandage from an attendant at the community stables facility that was hosting the event. Many of the young people attending the picnic had never been to such a place before. Their initially tentative and then more boisterous behavior reflected both their apprehension in new settings and their acuity for quickly adapting to new spaces. When I returned with the bandage, Sadiq, the young man with the knife wound, smiled appreciatively before carefully removing the old bandage and placing the new one over the hole in his leg. Tracey, meanwhile, stood in the distance, counseling a shy young woman who, like many other young women before her, had adopted Tracey as her "big sister." At times, the level of these girls' need overwhelmed Tracey, physically and emotionally. In addition to her commitment to her position as a program counselor, she was raising her own family, completing her undergraduate degree, and planning her wedding with the father of her young daughter and son. Sometimes, Tracey's frustration bubbled to the surface quickly, as it did in the car that fall afternoon.

In many ways, the final scene in the car encapsulates the theoretical and practical dilemmas I confronted while conducting field research with and on the Black community—an amorphous, diverse, and sometimes divided community—of which I consider myself a member. Stephanie's response to Tracey—"Nikki can represent it to them in their language"—suggests that I had adequately proven my ability to "code-switch" (Anderson 1999) and my ultimate loyalty to their side (see Becker 1967). Yet, although each of us identified as a Black woman, Tracey, Stephanie, and I represented three different sets of life experiences. Our experiences overlapped and diverged at the intersections of class, skin color, and sexuality. Over the course of three years, however, we were able to find a common ground that was defined at least in part by our identi-fication and experience as Black women.

But what does racial solidarity mean in our post–Civil Rights, post-apartheid, post-colonial world? Race scholar Howard Winant writes that today the concept of race is "more problematic than ever before"; racial identities in particular are "less solid and ineffable" than in earlier periods and they feature a "certain flexibility and fungibility" that is, Winant argues, unique to our era (2006, 987). Like other Black researchers who came before me—I was repeatedly inspired by Du Bois's *The Philadelphia Negro*, Drake and Cayton's *Black Metropolis*, Joyce Ladner's *Tomorrow's Tomorrow*, and Elijah Anderson's tril-ogy of ethnographic works—I found out that it takes more than skin color to guarantee solidarity. It also takes more than the right shade of skin color to earn the right to represent others. The urgency and significance of these points ebbed and flowed throughout my research and caused me alternating periods of anxiety and confidence familiar to many field researchers, regardless of race, gender, class, or sexuality.

Some of the questions that concerned me most during this time and still concern me today are those concerning represen-tation: Who am I to tell these stories about poor, Black girls? What rights did/do I have to represent their lives? Which stories do I tell and which do I leave out? What powers and problems characterize my attempt to represent these girls—and, in turn, myself—to others? In this appendix, I reflect critically on my experience as a light-skinned Black woman and doctoral candidate in her mid-twenties who was studying girls' fights. I focus this reflection on what I think of as the authenticity tests that I encountered during the first few months of the project, when much of my time was spent familiarizing myself with a group of intervention counselors who would facilitate my initial access to the teenaged girls and boys who are featured in this book. I reflect on the various challenges that emerged during my interactions with these counselors. I consider, as well, my relationship to the academy and the racialized and gendered dilemmas that I encountered, from the process of getting in to writing up this research.

ON GETTING IN, AUTHENTICITY, AND REPRESENTATION

In almost any sort of ethnographic endeavor, the field researcher occupies a strange position. She belongs and doesn't belong at the same time, and necessarily so. She is the "Simmelian stranger," that peculiar individual who is in the group, but not fully part of it; she is here today but may be gone tomorrow (Simmel 1971, 143). In occupying this position, the field researcher is open to certain confessions from her respondents, confidences that likely would not have been shared if the researcher had been a permanent member of the group. In my research, these confessional-like sessions sometimes ended in tears, as the strong, Black woman before me broke down. These episodes revealed what other girls and women I encountered and interviewed may not have stated explicitly on their own or in response to a survey question: even the toughest Black women and girls endure a tremendous amount of stress. They are, as I heard repeatedly over the years, "tired."

It was not only my position as a stranger that allowed or encouraged my respondents to open up to me in this way. In a racialized society such as ours, the stranger's skin color (and gender, class, sexual identity, and so on) influences and adds meaning to every social interaction. A sense of commonality, even trust, must be present before a person is likely to expose her or his vulnerability to a relative stranger, that is, to reveal what otherwise lingers in the back regions of one's life. How can such a trust develop in a matter of moments? How can this trust emerge in a setting where even the *idea* of trust is so tenuous? At these moments, it seemed to me, skin color and gender symbolized trust, connection, and solidarity. The Black women and girls I interviewed seemed to recognize that I was positioned in between their world and Whiteness—the *de facto* race of many of the social service institutions in their lives—and the combination of that distance and closeness, as signified by skin color and gender, helped to create a space where some teenaged girls felt they could share far more than they normally would with a person they did not know very well. It is here, in this shared intimacy of the field research experience, where I developed my perspective as an observant participant in—and of—the struggle that teenaged girls confronted in their everyday lives (Anderson 2001).[1]

The Intervention Team

Before gaining access to the backstage moments of inner-city girls' lives, I first had to negotiate and pass the many tests presented by members of the violence reduction program's intervention counseling team. Understanding the unique organizational and raced position of the team members requires first understanding something about the makeup and mission of the VRP. The program was developed by a group of doctors in response to their and their colleagues' frustration with the revolving door phenomenon: the constant flow of victims of youth violence in and out of the hospital's emergency rooms.

Overall, the program took a behavioral modification approach, which was then implemented by a team of intervention counselors. In the winter of 2001, when I made my initial contact, the intervention team had three members: Stephanie, Tracey, and Diana. Both Stephanie, who was the team supervisor, and Tracey are African American women who grew up in inner-city neighborhoods similar to where they were now working as VRP staff. Stephanie was in her late twenties and had worked in the city's community centers for several years. She lived in an integrated suburb north of the city. Her older sister and young nephew lived in South Philadelphia, a target area for the VRP, and she visited them there often. Tracey was in her early twenties and lived in West Philadelphia. She could walk to some of the VRP participants' homes to conduct interviews with these young people. Diana was thirty years old, a White woman from suburban Ohio who was (she admitted) unfamiliar with Philadelphia's inner-city neighborhoods and the life experiences of the youth she counseled. During the course of the project, other members joined the team as intervention counselors. Jimmy, a Puerto Rican man in his late twenties who had worked as a counselor in inner-city communities for the previous eight years, joined in the summer of 2001. Vince, an Asian American man in his early twenties who was raised in Philadelphia, and Syreeta, an African American woman in her early twenties who grew up in Philadelphia's Carver projects, also joined the team. Other than Diana, all members of the intervention counseling team were non-White and quite familiar with Philadelphia's inner-city neighborhoods.

In 2001, the VRP was housed in a small office in the city's children's hospital. The hospital was only steps away from the university where I attended graduate classes in sociology and criminology. The second-floor office was small and the three desks made the space seem especially crowded. During the first few weeks of the project, I visited the office regularly. During one of these visits, I asked Stephanie to describe how young people entered the project and to explain the design of the intervention. During our conversation, Stephanie began to talk about what she perceived as a fundamental problem with the intervention, namely that the tools designed to measure the risk of subsequent violence did not "speak to the population." When I asked her what she meant by that, she cited the importance of understanding both the local meanings used by young people and the range of social cues that might emerge during an interview. Subtle cues, such as a young person's choice of words or how she or he carried her- or himself, Stephanie emphasized, could provide a wealth of information, if the counselor was properly attuned. By the same token, key understandings about violence in these young people's lives were likely to be missed if these types of social cues went unheeded.

How do people learn about the significance of these informal codes, I wondered. "Can you train someone to be aware?" I asked Stephanie. In her opinion, this was not knowledge that could be gleaned simply from reading books. In fact, sometimes, book knowledge could interfere with an accurate assessment of what was going on in the lives of young people. Stephanie concluded from her experience working with kids in inner-city community centers that the best workers were often those with the least formal education. Personal experience with life in the inner city trumped formal education nearly every time.

AUTHENTICITY TESTS: "SHE'S NOT DIANA!"

During my first few months of field research, I discovered that the counselors often used perceived differences between street and book knowledge to distinguish outsiders from insiders on the intervention team. Team members also used other members' ability to demonstrate their "experience" to draw lines between insiders and outsiders. Since I was a relative stranger to the group, the intervention counselors, especially Tracey, spent a good deal of energy trying to categorize me. To them, I represented a special case: a Ph.D. student at an Ivy League university who was also a Black woman. In their efforts to place me, Tracey and others paid attention to how I spoke, the type of clothes I wore, and how I reacted to stories told about other counselors or members of the research team. Tracey's retelling of an encounter Diana, the only White counselor on the project, had had in the field, for example, helped her to evaluate my level of experience with the people in Philadelphia's inner-city neighborhoods.

I heard the story during a field visit in West Philadelphia. Tracey asked me if I had had a chance to go on a visit with Diana. I told her that I hadn't, but that I planned to accompany her soon. Tracey predicted that Diana would like me: "She'll be so happy [to have company]—she gets so nervous." When I asked Tracey what she meant, she responded with the following story. At the end of a recent visit Diana had made to the home of a program participant, the mother had walked Diana to the front door, said good-bye, and then added, "Be careful." "Be careful" or "be safe" are standard farewells used by people in the neighborhood. These types of farewells implicitly acknowledge the potential threats of the street, but they are not intended as warnings of immediate danger. Diana, however, took this good-bye as a warning. "You know how people say, 'Be careful' when you leave their house? Well, she took them seriously." According to Tracey, when Diana came back to the office, she told the other counselors that this interaction had made her very nervous. Next time she went on a visit, Diana announced, Stephanie or Tracey had to come with her. I laughed as I listened to the story.

In recounting this anecdote, Tracey made clear Diana's difference from the other members of the team. In addition, with the comment that I would "know how people say, 'Be careful,'" Tracey signaled that she assumed that I had access to the same type of knowledge that she did, and that I too would find Diana's concern comic. By laughing at the story, I verified this assumption. If I had not shared in Tracey's understanding of the situation, I would have seemed as ignorant of local life as Diana. If Tracey had concluded that I was more like Diana, and that I lacked the real-life experience the counselors valued over the book knowledge implied by my academic pedigree, then I would have likely been distanced from the group. In that case, my access to backstage conversations, neighborhood settings, and the young people whose stories would inform my project would have been quite limited.

During these first few months, each interaction with Tracey was a potential test of my familiarity with inner-city life. One such test of my street knowledge quickly became a running joke that strengthened my relationship with the team, especially Stephanie and Tracey. This test took place in a car when Tracey, Stephanie, Jimmy, and I were on the way to a home visit. During the ride, Tracey began to joke about how she was not going to be able to pay her rent that month, and so she planned to throw a house party. She would charge admission at the door to raise money for the rent. She paused before getting into the details of her plan and turned toward the back seat to address me. Using the deliberate speech of someone translating a foreign language, she began to explain to me what she meant by house party. Before she finished her definition, I interrupted, exclaiming, "I know what a goddamned house party is!" Everyone erupted in laughter. In a momentary lull, Tracey apologized for her assumption of my ignorance. Stephanie announced, "She's not Diana!" With obvious glee, Jimmy said, "Oh, we are having too much fun." Someone suggested I become an intervention counselor and we continued to laugh and joke about this until we arrived at the scheduled home visit.

My knowing the meaning of the term house party revealed information about me that was particularly important to these

counselors. Furthermore, that I would take offense (albeit jok-
ingly) at the presumption that I did not know the term provided the intervention counselors in the car with a clue about
who I really was in terms of class and experience, and was not.
In their eyes, I was a Black woman who possessed the book
knowledge valued by the doctors who developed the project,
but also the street knowledge valued by the intervention counselors. I knew enough to be on their side of the dividing line
between insiders and outsiders. Furthermore, I was certainly
not Diana, who represented the uninformed outsider whose
limited understanding of life on the streets had been gained in a
classroom setting. The significance of passing this test was not
lost on me. During the first year and a half of the study, the
intervention counseling team facilitated many of my field visits.
They would call me to coordinate visits to young people,
introduce me to various neighborhoods, and help me gain
access to other research sites. If the counselors had not trusted
me, or if they had found it difficult to interact with me, I
would have been forced to end the study not long after I had
begun it.

   In the weeks following the house party moment, the counselors became increasingly comfortable around me. They would
often joke that I should write a book about them, and not about
the young people in the project. An additional signal of my
inclusion in the group was that I became subject to the same
face-to-face teasing team members traded with one another. In
these back-and-forth exchanges, frequently initiated by Tracey,
class markers emerged as signs of within-group difference. For
instance, Tracey would sometimes point to my Kenneth Cole
shoes or leather backpack and announce to the group that I
must be secretly rich. She also made frequent references to my
ability to use and understand big words. Once, while preparing
for a workshop on violence intervention strategies, Tracey
remarked to Stephanie and Jimmy, "It'll be good if Nikki

comes. She can use all of her big words." This teasing revealed both my inclusion in the group and my distance—while I was a welcome member of the group, I was not necessarily one of them.

Repeatedly submitting to and passing these authenticity tests eventually had the desired cumulative effect. By the end of that first summer on the violence reduction project, I was accepted as part of the intervention team. I went on visits regularly; participated in project activities, including picnics, field trips, and holiday parties; and helped out in any other ways that seemed useful. I had little trouble coordinating visits with the counselors, and they were becoming more interested in helping me. At one point, when I was unable to make a visit, Tracey said the next day, "We missed you yesterday. That would have been a good visit for you." As the counselors grew increasingly comfortable with me, they also took a greater interest in what I was doing. During the early months of the project, when I was hanging out, observing, Tracey would often ask, "What are you doing?" At times I simply told her that I was documenting the intervention process. I usually added that I was also especially interested in what was going on with the young women and girls in the neighborhoods. Stephanie, Tracey, and I would often have conversations about what I was finding. We talked over lunch, during ride-alongs, as we rode the bus, or while we walked in the neighborhoods. These discussions helped to illuminate various aspects of the context of violence. The conversations also reinforced the counselors' general sense that other people involved with the project were unfamiliar with the context in which they were asking the intervention counselors to intervene. Both Stephanie and Tracey seemed to assume that my unique credentials—not simply my skin color but also my proven ability to pass their tests—would allow me to translate life on the streets to those who possessed more book knowledge and less street knowledge.

On Decency and Diversity

On that afternoon in the car when Tracey concluded, "Things are not going to change," both she and I were a bit tired of this representational dance. While I had proven my solidarity with her and her worldview, she did not necessarily believe that I would be able to effectively challenge or change the seemingly intractable ignorance of others who had much more power than she did. Tracey firmly believed that time and resources were regularly wasted because other people were unable or unwilling to recognize the diversity that existed within the inner-city community. "They think that all kids are alike," was how she frequently summed up her frustration. Once, as she and I were driving through her West Philadelphia neighborhood, returning from a farewell lunch for one of the intervention counselors, she addressed this subject at greater length. I often made use of times like this to test my working hypotheses about how young people negotiate conflict and violence in the inner-city setting. I suspect that Tracey always knew what I was doing, but she would listen patiently and offer her assessments or critiques, largely without reservation.

That afternoon, I offered the following observation for Tracey's consideration: "It seems like there is as a tension between the directors of this research project and the intervention counselors." At first, Tracey makes no response. Her exasperation is unmistakable, but the enormity of her frustration leaves her momentarily tongue-tied. Finally, she bursts out loudly, "All of these kids are not the same!" It is not until we near her home that Tracey finally reveals that the "real" reason the doctors cannot understand the existence of diversity in the population is, and "she hates to say the word," prejudice. The same lack of an in-depth understanding also informs how they think about the violence that occurs in the neighborhoods. I ask Tracey if she thinks the doctors' misperceptions represent a fundamental lack of understanding about fights, in particular, about their seriousness and their consequences. "Oh yes! You get into a fight and they think your life is over. And don't get into one fight and have come from a single-parent family—then you going to be a serial killer."

Tracey and I continue to talk about prejudice and stereotyping as we approach her house. "Like that street there," I say, pointing to a typical block off Baltimore Avenue as a way to test Tracey's assertions, "they will think that everyone on that block is the same, when actually there is a diversity of people there." Tracey nods in silent affirmation.

"If you know," I add, "you know."

"And the same is true in the suburbs," she notes before challenging the necessity of insider knowledge as a basis for knowing one's fellow human beings: "Even if you don't know, you *should* know."

It is this inability of others to understand and to view Black people as something other than a monolithic mass of similarly situated human beings that frustrated Tracey from the beginning of the project to this day in the car. This frustration, of course, is quite familiar to Black scholars. Patricia Hill Collins describes what may be the roots of Tracey's frustration in *Black Sexual Politics* (2004): "Racial segregation, however, has created large numbers of white Americans who lack sustained, personal experience with African Americans. This group routinely must be convinced of Black humanity, a task that requires that they jettison racial stereotypes and learn to see and value Blacks as individuals" (2004, 15).

Although Tracey's knowledge of the diversity in the target population is informed by her understanding of her own community, observers less directly involved have reached similar conclusions. Nearly every rigorous ethnographic observation of the ghetto, slum, or inner-city community has recognized the existence of social systems based on hierarchical classification schemes. Three of the most notable discussions of the local hierarchies of Black communities are found in Du Bois's *The Philadelphia Negro*, Drake and Cayton's *Black Metropolis*, and Anderson's *Code of the Street*. Du Bois, writing more than a hundred years ago, observed:

> There is always a strong tendency on the part of the community to consider the negroes as composing one practically homogenous mass. This view has of course a certain justification: the people of Negro descent in this land have had a common history, suffer to-day common disabilities, and contribute to one general set of social problems. And yet if the foregoing statistics have emphasized any one fact it is that wide variations in antecedents, wealth, intelligence, and general efficiency have already been differentiated within this group . . . and there is no surer way of misunderstanding the Negro or being misunderstood by him than by ignoring manifest differences of condition and power in the 40,000 black people of Philadelphia. ([1899] 1996, 310)

As Du Bois suggests, class divisions within the Black community are not mere abstractions created by observers; local residents also acknowledge these distinctions.[2] In his study of contemporary Philadelphia's inner-city neighborhoods, Anderson found similarly important distinctions between Black people in Philadelphia nearly a century after Du Bois's discovery.

Those of us with academic training or a healthy sociological imagination would likely trace Tracey's frustration to larger patterns of social segregation and racism. Tracey's appreciation of the diversity in the inner-city community, however, is not informed by this kind of "book knowledge." Her worldview is rooted in her lived experience—certainly, she knows where she is located in the social typology of the inner city—and her deep belief in the humanity of all people. After three years of work with the VRP, she is no longer sure that anyone is adequately positioned to make others understand the diversity of the community she serves. In the following section, I turn from Tracey's frustration with the challenges of representation to my own challenges in "enlightening" others.

(RE)TELLING STORIES: FROM IGNORANCE TO ENLIGHTENMENT

"People remember stories," is advice that field researcher Howard Becker once passed along during a visit to a graduate seminar I attended. This insight deeply informs how I represent my work in public presentations and in writing. "What is the story?" I now ask my students who are conducting field research projects. The stories are important, I tell them. Yet, in the academy, just like in the rest of social life, we tell our ethnographic tales in a social context that is informed by race, gender, class, and power. In recent years, who gets to tell these stories and how they are told has started to receive critical attention.[3] As a graduate student, and now as an assistant professor, I have wrestled with the racialized gender politics that determines who gets to tell stories about poor, Black people and how their stories are told. I began to think critically about the structure of the ethnographic tale after I began receiving comments from others about how I told my story about inner-city girls and violence. Several people commented that I represented the girls' story in such a matter-of-fact way. As I reflected on these comments and continued to read the most popular ethnographies in the field, I began to see that some people seemed to be most struck by what was *missing* from my story.

In an attempt to explain the inner workings of one group of people to another, many contemporary ethnographic texts begin from a point of ignorance instead of from a point of understanding or commonality. This ignorance may be real or, more likely (I hope), feigned in an attempt to connect with a certain audience. For example, otherwise progressive scholars may ask questions about poor women's mothering choices in an attempt to hook the more conservative policy makers and voters among us. While this may be an effective storytelling strategy (the continuing attacks on poor mothers and women of color make this presumed effectiveness questionable, however), assuming a veil of ignorance seems to result in an end almost diametrically opposed to what most liberal or progressive researchers intend their work to achieve. Many scholars aim to move their readers from a state of ignorance to one of enlightenment with the hope that once enlightenment is reached policymakers or voters or other benevolent stakeholders will do the right thing. However, adopting an ideological framework, especially one that is inherently racist and misogynistic, in an attempt to enlighten those with the power to effect change can—and, I would argue, often does—have the effect of making the others under study *more* unintelligible than they ever really were. Such a storytelling strategy may produce sympathy for a particular group; it is much less likely to evoke empathy— a deep and shared understanding of the lived experiences of others.

Mitchell Duneier describes the style of storytelling that I allude to here in his award-winning *Slim's Table*: "Sociology, like many disciplines today, is constituted of some scholars who tend to function as politically correct stereotype guardians. They say, 'You are guilty of carrying around an unenlightened, negative image of blacks. But you can depend upon me, in my innocence and enlightenment, to set you straight'" (1992, 138). Duneier traces his own racial enlightenment to classic field studies of Black life (he cites Drake and Cayton's *Black Metropolis*, Elliot Liebow's *Tally's Corner*, Ulf Hannerz's *Soulside*, and Elijah Anderson's *A Place on the Corner* and *Streetwise*, among others). "In discussing the urban ethnographic tradition," he writes, "I immediately recall how much more enlightened I felt after some of my own gross stereotypes about blacks were transcended through an encounter with these works" (139). Duneier's honest disclosure and critique reveal the importance of interrogating the assumptions and perspectives that we bring to our research. I came to my research with a set of assumptions and presumptions that influenced how I went about my work and, ultimately, how I represented this work. Some of these initial assumptions were challenged. Yet, it is important to distinguish between everyday assumptions and feigned or willful ignorance. In light of Duneier's analysis, I cannot honestly say that I began my research from either ignorance or innocence.

In contrast to the perspective apparent in many popular ethnographic works on Black populations, I began this research confident that the humanity of Black people was not a subject for debate. Like Tracey, I know of the diversity within the Black community and I have some appreciation of the lived implications of these differences. Patricia Hill Collins makes a similar point in *Black Sexual Politics*, where she writes, "For me, evidence for the humanity of Black people lies in the beauty of Black individualism. In all of my work, this has been *my starting point, not my destination*" (emphasis mine; 2004, 15).

I am sure that well-intentioned scholars think that they are indeed breaking down stereotypes and humanizing their subjects by telling ethnographic tales in this way, that is, by translating the lives of "others" in a way that makes them understandable to some other—*and this is the real paradox*—better educated and more privileged yet still ignorant group of people. However, I wonder if in taking this approach, scholars participate in the kind of dehumanization they are trying to challenge. One could argue, for example, that taking up the task of proving one group's humanity to another group is just as dehumanizing as questioning that claim to humanity at all. Ultimately, what such an approach tells us is the all too familiar story about the position and politics of a particular researcher and her public audience. It does not deliver the story.

"TELL IT"

In the end, it is the story and the stories that matter. Most field researchers get to the story in a similar way. They become interested in a particular group of people; they spend time with the group, listening, hanging out, and taking copious field notes. They systematically review and analyze the notes and gradually develop a theory about what is happening in a particular setting or with a particular group of people. After years of this work, the story finally emerges—or is pulled—from this mound of data. Yet, discovering the story is only half of the work. You must also tell it.[4]

A final challenge that I want to consider briefly here is the politics—disciplinary, ideological, and personal—of *where* stories get told. One of the biggest challenges in telling this story about poor, Black girls' use of aggression and violence was the preexisting context in which the story would be heard— one in which hypermasculinized images of Black girls were already in circulation. There was little space within urban sociology to tell this tale because much of that literature is concerned with the experience of young, Black men.[5] Arguably, more writing on Black women and girls is available in the criminological literature than in sociology. Yet, I did not encounter the girls in this study in a delinquent or criminal context. Where then, I wondered, would I be able to tell their stories?

This challenge was highlighted in a set of reviewers' comments I received from a journal that is sensitive to feminist writings and research on gender. The reviewers recommended that I revise and resubmit this piece and instructed me to resituate my discussion squarely in the *criminological* literature on gender and crime, *instead* of in the urban sociology of Elijah Anderson or the Black feminist thought of Patricia Hill Collins. As I read these instructions I was somewhat discouraged to learn that in spite of the advances made by women and feminists in the discipline, the same challenges that Joyce Ladner encountered decades ago in writing her study of poor, Black girls in St. Louis remained. In her introduction to the paperback edition of *Tomorrow's Tomorrow*, "A Twenty-five-Year Retrospective," she explains, "[W]riting *Tomorrow's Tomorrow* was my attempt to reconceptualize the 'deviance/pathology' model of black family life and black women and see them as resourceful, normal women who were simply trying to cope with some of the harsher conditions of life. What other scholars had traditionally viewed as weaknesses and pathologies, I chose to view as strength and coping strategies in dealing with stress" (1995, xii). In the end, I resisted (and continue to resist) others' attempts to label the girls in this study as offenders, victims, delinquents, or criminals, primarily because the evidence does not support such claims. Girls' lives are not contained in these labels. Furthermore, the language that girls use to describe themselves holds far more descriptive and explanatory power than the labels that others would force upon them. These girls are good girls, pretty girls, sometimes violent girls, and fighters who are deeply involved in a struggle for survival.

My efforts to find ways to tell this story my way sometimes leave me as frustrated and tired as Tracey was in the car that afternoon. The challenges of representation are as real in the academy as they are in the field. In both settings we must pass tests and make the choices—personal, political, and ideological—that will determine if and how the story gets told.

Notes

Introduction

1. I have renamed this high school and surrounding buildings to preserve respondents' confidentiality and anonymity. I have made similar changes throughout the text. All names in this book are pseudonyms.

2. I visited these places between 2001 and 2004 in various roles, including as a graduate research assistant (Jones 2004b), a research consultant for a study of girls in Philadelphia's juvenile detention center, a student in an introductory criminal justice class at a men's maximum-security prison, and a co-instructor for the same course for women in the city's jail. See *Criminalizing the Classroom: The Over-Policing of New York City Schools*, a report based on one thousand student surveys and the analysis of publicly available data, conducted by the New York Civil Liberties Union and the Racial Justice Program of the American Civil Liberties Union, for students' accounts of how an increased police presence influences the school setting (2007, 11–19).

3. A fair one typically refers to a staged fight with agreed-upon rules, for example, fists only. The terms "rolled on" or "jumped" typically describe surprise attacks involving a group.

4. In *American Apartheid: Segregation and the Making of the Underclass*, Massey and Denton describe the consequences of concentrated poverty and racial segregation: "By building decay, crime, and social disorder into the residential structure of black communities, segregation creates a harsh and extremely disadvantaged environment to which ghetto blacks must adapt. In concentrating poverty, moreover, segregation also concentrates conditions such as drug use, joblessness, welfare dependency, teenage childbearing, and unwed parenthood, producing a social context where these conditions are not only common but the norm" (1993, 13). For a discussion of how social isolation influences violent crime in segregated communities see Ruth D. Peterson and Lauren J. Krivo's "Macrostructural analyses of race, ethnicity, and violent crime: Recent lessons and new directions for research" (2005) and

Lauren J. Krivo and Ruth D. Peterson's "Racial segregation and Black urban homicide" (1993).

5. The poverty threshold for the 2000 U.S. Census was $8,501 in annual income for one person (aged 65 and under) and $16,954 for a family of four ("Poverty: 1999, Census 2000 Brief," issued May 2003).

6. I use the terms "African American" and "Black" interchangeably throughout the book. Respondents and residents typically used these terms interchangeably too. These terms do not reflect natural or essential differences between human beings; rather, these are socially constructed terms that reflect people's place on a racial hierarchy. Of course, these terms also hold great cultural and political meaning. In *From Black Power to Hip Hop*, Patricia Hill Collins explains that she uses "the term 'Black women' deliberately, because I feel that there is a pressing need for a unifying language that women of African descent and women who are rendered socially Black can use to describe their needs as racial/ethnic women" (2006, 23).

7. See chapter 2 for a discussion of how one teenaged girl I interviewed developed distrust of the police over the course of a year. See also Fine et al.'s "'Anything can happen with police around': Urban youth evaluate strategies of surveillance" (2003) and Daiute and Fine's "Youth perspectives on violence and injustice" (2003) for a discussion of the perceptions youth hold of law enforcement.

8. Anderson summarizes the relationship between neighborhood circumstances and the use of violence in a recent National Institute of Justice Research Brief (Stewart and Simons 2009) that validates much of Anderson's original thesis: "The inclination to violence springs from the circumstances of life among the ghetto poor—the lack of jobs that pay a living wage, the stigma of race, the fallout from rampant drug use and drug trafficking, and the resulting alienation and lack of hope for the future. Simply living in such an environment places young people at special risk of falling victim to aggressive behavior." The report "emphasizes the need to consider this theory in future studies within African American households, neighborhoods, and communities" (ii).

9. This form of manhood is not unique to urban men, as Patricia Hill Collins writes in *Black Sexual Politics* (2004). White men with wealth and power also demonstrate a masculinity that combines strength and dominance, for example, through economic or military, in addition to physical, dominance. Poor Black men who live in distressed urban areas and are blocked from other resources to display their manhood too often come to rely on *physical* domination, which makes themselves and others in their community more vulnerable to violent victimization. Anderson's and Collins's analyses are consistent with masculinity studies that describe how the

lack of access to economic resources encourages poor men of color to "become men" through displays of physical strength and violence. See also Connell and Messerschmidt (2005) for a comprehensive review of this work and *Gender Talk: The Struggle for Women's Equality in African American Communities* (Cole and Guy-Sheftall 2003) for further discussion of Black gender ideology.

10. See "Gender, streetlife, and criminal retaliation" (Mullins, Wright, and Jacobs 2004) for an in-depth analysis of how gender structures expectations of retaliation and vengeance in the criminal street networks of St. Louis. See also "Retaliatory homicide: Concentrated disadvantage and neighborhood crime" (Kubrin and Weitzer 2003).

11. I examine similarities and differences in how girls and boys work the code of the street in "Working 'the code': On girls, gender, and inner-city violence" (Jones 2008). Jody Miller examines how gender influences girls' involvement in gangs, including the use of interpersonal violence across gang-involved and non-gang-involved youth, in *One of the Guys: Girls, Gangs, and Gender* (2001). Miller also describes how gender shapes the accomplishment of street robbery in "Up it up: Gender and the accomplishment of street robbery" (1998).

12. West and Zimmerman describe this ongoing, interactional process as "doing gender": "Doing gender means creating differences between girls and boys and women and men, differences that are not natural, essential, or biological" (1987, 137).

13. Michelle Obama and the first family have recently replaced the fictional Huxtables as the most recognizable Black middle-class family.

14. The salience of "the Black lady" as a familiar image for adolescent girls was revealed in how some respondents described me to others. For example, girls often described me (a light-skinned Black woman with short, naturally curly hair and an urban, middle-class demeanor) to others as "a lady" or "the violence lady." The shop owner I describe in the preface to this book also uses the term "lady" to describe me to someone on the phone.

15. As with other terms that are popular in youth cultures, the term "ghetto" has multiple meanings and can be used in ways that reinforce and challenge the pejorative meanings that circulate in popular culture.

16. Youth who were injured in domestic violence or who were victims of child abuse were not eligible for participation in the program. Once enrolled in VRP, a random sample of youth was assigned to receive intervention from a team of counselors who, over the course of several months, visited the young people in their homes, offered referrals, and provided mentoring, interventions designed to reduce the risk of subsequent violence. I was hired by the VRP to provide qualitative documentation of this intervention process.

Additional background information about the violence reduction program is available in the appendix.

17. I use "stages" and "phases" here in order to signal the different streams of data collection that took place over the three-year course of the project, but in practice, some aspects of these phases overlapped and/or flowed into one another. For example, I conducted my first in-depth interviews with Danielle, Terrie, and Amber toward the end of the second phase and continued to follow up with them throughout the third and final phase of the project.

18. I have included a methodological appendix that considers the politics of ethnographic representation. I discuss and critically evaluate what was involved in situating myself as a light-skinned Black woman in academia in her mid-twenties who was studying "girls' fights." I describe how I presented myself to the violence reduction program counselors who facilitated my initial fieldwork. I consider, in particular, my relationship to the academy and the racialized, classed, and gendered challenges and dilemmas that I encountered, from the process of "getting in" to "writing up" this research.

19. This sub-sample was generated randomly from the intervention program participant list. Seventeen of the interviews were audiotaped, using a microcassette recorder. The profiles in this book are drawn from interviews, observations, and conversations with these and other VRP participants over this time.

20. I recorded my encounters and interviews with Terrie, Danielle, and Amber in my field notes and, at times, using a microcassette recorder. I analyzed the interviews with Terrie, Danielle, and Amber, as well as the interviews conducted during the second phase of the study, using the method of analytic induction. Howard Becker (1998, 195) explains analytic induction this way:

> When you do analytic induction, you develop and test your theory case by case. You formulate an explanation for the first case as soon as you have gathered data on it. You apply that theory to the second case when you get data on it. If the theory explains that case adequately, thus confirming the theory, no problem; you go on to the third case. When you hit a "negative case," one your explanatory hypothesis doesn't explain, you change the explanation of what you're trying to explain, by incorporating into it whatever new elements the facts of this troublesome case suggest to you, or else you change the definition of what you're going to explain as to exclude the recalcitrant case from the universe of things to be explained.

21. Elijah Anderson describes the subtle distinction "between the 'participant observer' and the 'observant participant.' The former may be in an early, tentative process of negotiating a relationship with the group under study, and may be satisfied with this position,

while the latter has become close to the subjects, effectively empathizing with them, and it is hoped, able to articulate their point of view" (2001, 35).

22. For a recent study of this problem see *Getting Played: African American Girls, Urban Inequality, and Gendered Violence* (Miller 2008).

CHAPTER 1. THE SOCIAL WORLD OF INNER-CITY GIRLS

1. Patricia Hill Collins describes "othermothers" as "women who assist bloodmothers by sharing mothering responsibilities" and as a defining element of mothering in Black communities (1990, 119).

2. Various studies suggest that women in general are less likely than men to use guns. My research supports those claims. Once involved in the drug trade, however, a woman is subject to the same types of violence as a man and is likely to be involved in the same sort of violent disputes as men. Women in the drug trade are also more vulnerable to sexual violence than their male counterparts. See Lisa Maher's *Sexed Work: Gender, Race and Resistance in a Brooklyn Drug Market* (1997) for a discussion of women's use of violence in drug markets.

3. Patricia Hill Collins also explains the "visionary pragmatism" of Black mothers, grandmothers, and othermothers who socialized Black girls for survival under oppressive conditions: "African American mothers place a strong emphasis on protections, either by trying to shield their daughters as long as possible from the penalties attached to their derogated status or by teaching them skills of independence and self-reliance" (2000, 186). See also Janie Victoria Ward's "Raising resisters: The role of truth telling in the psychological development of African American girls" (1996) for an example of how Black mothers pass along survival lessons to their daughters.

4. While Black feminist scholars and some researchers have written on Black mothers' efforts to socialize their daughters for survival, little has been said about how changing threats to girls' well-being, especially the threat of interpersonal violence, affects African American girls' relationships with their peers.

5. One of the most dramatic violent events, the "Lex Street Massacre," occurred shortly before I began my field research in Philadelphia. Seven people were killed in the December 28 crack house killing, the largest mass murder in the city's history. See "A long painful decline: West Philadelphia's Mill Creek has suffered neglect for years. Residents live in fear of the kind of violence that erupted last month" (Kinney and Boyer 2001) and "Life led 10 people into a crack house; 7 never made it out. It was the city's worst mass murder. They got 'caught in the madness,'" (Zucchino and Kinney 2001).

6. Marjorie Harness Goodwin provides a comprehensive analysis of what Shante describes as the "he say/she say" in *He-Said-She-Said: Talk as Social Organization among Black Children* (1990).

CHAPTER 2. "IT'S NOT WHERE YOU LIVE, IT'S HOW YOU LIVE"

1. A medical student accompanied me on this visit, observing from the side for most of the interview.
2. The hairstyles that Black women choose hold personal, political, and cultural meaning. In inner-city settings, getting a "good" perm signals economic status. "Good" perms are relatively expensive, costing upwards of $65 per treatment. Properly straightened hair, even if it is not done professionally, is an acceptable alternative. Some girls "know how to press" their own hair because they have been taught this much-admired skill by their mothers, grandmothers, or aunties (see Banks 2000, 21).
3. Hip-hop music and videos offer a constellation of competing, contradictory, and controlling images. Rappers like Li'l Kim, who identifies as a feminist, assert themselves in ways that both mirror and manipulate gendered expectations. Yet, hip-hop is also dominated by degrading images of Black femininity and Black masculinity (Collins 2004; Sharpley-Whiting 2007).
4. See "Get your freak on: Sex, babies, and images of Black femininity" in *Black Sexual Politics* (Collins 2004, 119–148).
5. See Anderson 1999 and Ness 2004.
6. Lyn Mikel Brown discusses a case of this kind of "jealousy" in her study of betrayal and rejection among adolescent girls. See *Girlfighting* (2003). Julie Bettie also includes an example of what I describe as the "she thinks she's all that" argument in her book *Women without Class* (2003).
7. In describing girls' survival strategies as "situated" I am drawing on Kevin Roy's ethnographic analysis of fatherhood in Chicago neighborhoods (2004). Roy offers that fatherhood is located in physical and social spaces, and explains how the presence of gangs, police activity, and poverty influences how, where, and when men perform fatherhood duties. Girls' survival strategies are also "situated" in this way, that is, they are grounded in the physical and social ecology of distressed urban neighborhoods. Adolescent girls' management of violence is intertwined with their concerns about survival in these settings. A similar concern with "survival" was reported in DeKeseredy et al.: "In the qualitative interviews [with women in public housing], many women reported that they were concerned with 'survival,' and their main strategy is to mind their own business and refuse to acknowledge problems or report crime." (2003, 16). Furthermore, these survival strategies are of a

different nature from those discussed in Carol Stack's *All Our Kin* (1974). The trust-based networks of poor, Black neighborhoods have been under serious stress over the last several decades, resulting in decreased levels of reported collective efficacy (for example, see Sampson, Raudenbush, and Earls 1997).

8. Katherine Irwin also found that adolescents living in a range of impoverished Denver, Colorado, neighborhoods turned to friends and avoided people or places to manage threats of violence in these settings (2004). For research on adolescent girls' use of relational aggression see *Aggression, Antisocial Behavior, and Violence among Girls* (Putallaz and Bierman 2004). See also "Policing girlhood? Relational aggression and violence prevention" (Chesney-Lind, Morash, and Irwin 2007) for a review and critique of the relational aggression literature.

CHAPTER 3. "AIN'T I A VIOLENT PERSON?"

1. For a description of this program see http://www.temple.edu/inside-out/. Block names have been changed.
2. A medical student accompanied me on this visit, observing from the side for most of the interview.
3. See Tricia Rose's *Black Noise: Rap Music and Black Culture in Contemporary America* (1994) for a discussion of women's participation in hip-hop. See also Charis E. Kubrin's "Gangstas, thugs, and hustlas: Identity and the code of the street in rap music" (2005).
4. Of course, there are a number of ways to adapt to being an outsider. Using the prism of aggression and violence shows just one set of adaptations to an outsider identity.
5. It is difficult to say how this relates to self-esteem. It may be that acquiring a special-status position as an outsider increases one's level of self-esteem. It is also possible that the stress associated with always being on may complicate the development of healthy levels of self-esteem in some urban, adolescent girls.
6. An adolescent girl who attends an urban public school sums up how girls work to maintain their reputations as fighters: "So if you want to stay hard, you gotta fight to stay hard" (respondent quoted in Brown 2003, 169).
7. Girls' appreciation and even desire for this sort of respect and power has received very little attention from scholars. Studies that do address fighting sometimes assume that teenaged girls who engage in physical fights and the expressive machinations that surround them are simply trying to be "like" boys. In *Girlfighting*, for example, Lyn Mikel Brown argues, "Girls who don't want to be associated with weakness and vulnerability end up *modeling* or *posing* macho toughness and bravado" (2003, 171; emphasis added). The girl fighters I interviewed and spent time with were committed to

their public personas as fighters; they were not "posing." Such an interpretation fails to acknowledge the real sense of power that girls who say they "like" to fight or are good at fighting derive from being able to handle themselves.

8. Audre Lorde's discussion of the transformation of feeling and emotion into action, along with her essay on the uses of anger were instructive in my efforts to understand and articulate the adolescent, inner-city girls' struggle for respect, power, and mobility (1984). Feminist criminologist Sally Simpson, drawing on the Black feminist thought of Patricia Hill Collins and Audre Lorde, points out that for African American girls and women, "Living daily with the fact of violence leads to an incorporation of it into one's experiential self. *Men, women, and children* have to come to terms with, make sense of, and respond to violence as it penetrates their lives" (Simpson 1991, 128–129; emphasis mine).

9. See *From Invisible to Incorrigible: The Demonization of Marginalized Women and Girls* (Chesney-Lind and Eliason 2006).

10. "A correctly staged and performed scene leads the audience to impute a self to a performed character, but this imputation—this self—*is a product of a scene that comes off, and is not a cause of it*. The self, then, as a performed character is not an organic thing that has a specific location, whose fundamental fate is to be born, to mature and to die; it is a dramatic effect arising diffusely from a scene that is presented, and the characteristic issue, the crucial concern, is whether it will be credited or discredited" (Goffman 1959, 253; emphasis mine).

CHAPTER 4.   "LOVE MAKE YOU FIGHT CRAZY"

1. See "When violence hits home: How economics and neighborhood play a role" (National Institute of Justice 2004) for a discussion of the increased likelihood of victimization for African American women living in economically disadvantaged neighborhoods.

2. I discuss similar strategies used by incarcerated Black women in "A bad relationship: Violence in the lives of incarcerated Black women" (Jones 2004b).

3. In *NO! The Rape Documentary* (2001), Aishah Simmons provides a compelling account of Black women's experiences with rape and the complexity of Black women's responses to sexual assault. For resources on sexual assault, see http://notherapedocumentary.org/.

4. Poor women in general, and poor Black women in particular, are less likely than are women in other social positions to actively seek out the public and private resources that have become available for battered and abused women in recent decades. For an analysis of intimate violence in public housing projects see "Public housing

and domestic violence" (Raphael 2001); "'Private' crime in public housing: Violent victimization, fear of crime and social isolation among women public housing residents" (Renzetti and Maier 2002); and "Perceived collective efficacy and women's victimization in public housing" (DeKeseredy et al. 2003).

5. While Lacy does not describe this man as a "stalker," her experience, as she described it to me, conforms closely to the legal definition of stalking. The following excerpt is taken from Pennsylvania's stalking statute (18 Pa.C.S. § 2709.1. Amended 2002; for the full text, see http://www.ncvc.org/src/main.aspx?dbID=DB_Pennsylvania206).

(a) Offense Defined.—A person commits the crime of stalking when the person either: (1) engages in a course of conduct or repeatedly commits acts toward another person, including following the person without proper authority, under circumstances which demonstrate either an intent to place such other person in reasonable fear of bodily injury or to cause substantial emotional distress to such other person; or (2) engages in a course of conduct or repeatedly communicates to another person under circumstances which demonstrate or communicate either an intent to place such other person in reasonable fear of bodily injury or to cause substantial emotional distress to such other person.

6. For a critical analysis of how intersections of race, gender, and class shaped the mainstream domestic violence movement see Crenshaw 1995.

7. See also *In Search of Respect: Selling Crack in El Barrio* (Bourgois 2002) for a discussion of violence against women in drug markets.

8. Amber told me that the agency did not remove Amber or her sister from the home because the girls' primary caretakers were their aunt and grandmother, not their mother.

9. Mary Pattillo's commentary (2006) on *Promises I Can Keep: Why Poor Women Put Motherhood before Marriage* by Kathryn Edin and Maria Kefalas (2005) emphasized the importance of the distinction between having a baby *by* someone and having a baby *with* someone.

10. Amber will have to take her relationship with Marvin into consideration in all future life decisions. For example, she has not filed for child support but may do so if her economic situation worsens. She will also have to consider his response if she develops a serious relationship with another man who will help raise Keenan. In this sense, even if a young woman and her baby's father are not together, she still has to account for him.

11. See Dorothy Robert's *Killing the Black Body: Race, Reproduction, and the Meaning of Liberty* (1998) for an analysis of race and reproductive control of Black women's bodies, including a discussion on the distribution of Depo-Provera in poor Black communities.

Conclusion

1. See Segura 1986 for a discussion of "triple oppression."
2. In her discussion of Black "bloodmothers, othermothers, and women-centered networks," Patricia Hill Collins notes, "Grandmothers, sisters, aunts or cousins act as othermothers by taking on child-care responsibilities for one another's children. Historically, when needed, temporary child-care arrangements often turned into long-term care or informal adoption (Stack 1974; Gutman 1976). These practices continue [today] in the face of changing social pressures" (Collins 2000, 179). See also Anderson's detailed ethnographic account of the challenges facing grandmothers who raise young people in the inner-city setting (1999, 206–236). See also France Winddance Twine's description of "racial literacy" lessons that white mothers pass along to their biracial children (2004).
3. Black feminist and gender scholars and Black women writers have explained how the material circumstances of poor women's lives in general and poor Black women in particular have often required a commitment to raising and becoming "strong" women. Black women's embrace and expression of strength contrast with mainstream (White) conceptions of femininity that place formal and informal limits on women's use of physical aggression: "Black women have long struggled with the behavioral dimensions of femininity whereby the very characteristics of femininity were neither *possible* nor desirable" (Collins 2004, 197; emphasis mine). The "passivity" and "submissiveness" that are considered benchmarks of hegemonic (White) femininity, for example, were "never in the cards for us [Black women]"; instead, "independence and resiliency," seemingly "masculine" traits were "admired" and acted out by many Black women "because they aided in the collective survival" of the community (Gloria Naylor, as quoted in Collins 2004, 197). See also Collins 2000, Lorde 1984, and Ladner 1971.
4. In *Compelled to Crime: The Gender Entrapment of Battered Black Women*, Beth Richie writes: "Every day in this country some women are coerced or forced by circumstances into doing things they don't want to do. For many women, it is the only static condition of their ever changing lives: to regularly feel required to make hard choices among, at times, very poor options. This situation forces some of us to assume a posture in the world that isn't in our best interest, or we betray ourselves for the good of others by acting in ways or living in relationships that don't serve us well." (1996, 1).
5. Still, gender differences in working the code do exist. These differences are rooted in the relationships between masculinity, femininity, and the use of violence or aggression in distressed urban areas,

and they emerge from the overlapping and intersecting survival and gender projects. See Jones 2008 for a discussion of intergender differences in the working of the code.

6. In this book, I am concerned with how inner-city girls negotiate racialized gender ideologies and cultural codes that govern interpersonal violence in the inner city; however, we can easily imagine similar efforts at reconciling competing and contradictory systems of accountability in other settings, from the corporate boardroom to the United States Congress. Everett C. Hughes' early examination of "the lady engineer" (1945) is useful in considering how such dilemmas are reconciled.

7. The consideration of gender similarities and differences in recent qualitative and theoretical work on violence and aggression has provided important insights and has drawn attention to significant theoretical concerns (Miller 2001, 1998; Heimer and De Coster 1999; Maher 1997), yet, little of this work is informed by a Black feminist perspective. In contrast, feminist criminologists Meda Chesney-Lind and Sally Simpson have provided nuanced analyses of violence and the criminalization of girls' survival strategies.

8. In a study of teenaged girls she conducted twenty-five years after *Tomorrow's Tomorrow*, Joyce Ladner acknowledges this change. She writes: "[T]heir [poor, Black teenaged girls in Washington, DC] poverty was overwhelming, their kinship networks were fewer, hence they suffered from more social isolation than did the girls in the original study" ([1971] 1995, xiii).

9. In "Copper Brown and Blue Black: Colorism and Self Evaluation," Thompson and Keith provide the following definition of colorism: "Colorism embodies preference and desire for both light skin as well as those other attendant features. Hair, eye color and facial features function, along with color in complex ways, to shape opportunities, norms regarding attractiveness, self concept, and overall body image" (2004).

Appendix

1. There are a number of ways in which intersections of race, gender, class, and sexuality can influence the researcher-respondent relationship. See Winddance and Warren's *Racing Research, Researching Race: Methodological Dilemmas in Critical Race Studies* (2000).

2. In *Black Metropolis*, Drake and Cayton write:
Everybody in Bronzeville recognizes the existence of social classes, whether called that or not. People with slight education, small incomes, and few of the social graces are always referring to the more affluent and successful as "dicties," "stuck-ups," "muckti-mucks," "high-toned folks," "tony people." The "strainers" and "strivers" are well-recognized

social types, people whose whole lives are dominated by the drive to get ahead and who show it by conspicuous consumption and a persistent effort to be seen with the right people and in the right places. People at the top of the various pyramids that we have described are apt to characterize people below them as "low-class," "trash," "riff-raff," "shiftless." The highly sensitive professional and business classes, keenly aware of the estimate which the white world puts on Negro behavior, frequently complain that white people do not recognize the class distinctions within the Negro community. ([1945] 1993, 521) Everett and Helen Hughes also comment on this seemingly universal tendency for individuals in a society to distinguish themselves from others, and the "inner drama" involved in doing so: "In all societies, individuals are classified, and thereby differentiated as to social fate. Some of the categories are easy to escape from; others are not. People of some categories have more power and are treated with greater deference than those of others; status connotes rank" (1952, 101).

3. For a recent example of this critique see the *American Journal of Sociology* Review Symposium "Scrutinizing the Street: Poverty, Morality, and the Pitfalls of Urban Ethnography" by Loïc Wacquant (2002) and with responses from Mitchell Duneier, Elijah Anderson, and Katherine Newman.

4. Throughout the writing process, Elijah Anderson repeatedly reminded me of the dual nature of my responsibilities. I needed first to discover the story, he would say, and then to "tell it."

5. I also found great encouragement in the work of Michelle Fine and Niobe Way, whose research has examined urban girls' lives with deep insight and sensitivity.

References

Anderson, Elijah. 2001. Urban ethnography. In *International encyclopedia of the social and behavioral sciences*, ed. Neil J. Smelser and Paul B. Baltes. Oxford: Pergamon Press.

———. 1999. *Code of the street: Decency, violence, and the moral life of the inner city*. New York: W.W. Norton.

———. 1994. The code of the street. *Atlantic Monthly*, May.

———. 1990. *Streetwise: Race, class and change in an urban community*. Chicago: University of Chicago Press.

———. 1978. *A place on the corner*. Chicago: University of Chicago Press.

Banks, Ingrid. 2000. *Hair matters: Beauty, power, and black women's consciousness*. New York: New York University Press.

Becker, Howard S. 1998. *Tricks of the trade: How to think about your research while you're doing it*. Chicago: University of Chicago Press.

———. 1967. Whose side are we on? *Social Problems* 14, no. 3 (Winter): 239–247.

Bettie, Julie. 2003. *Women without class: Girls, race, and identity*. Berkeley and Los Angeles: University of California Press.

Bourgois, Phillipe. 2002. *In search of respect: Selling crack in El Barrio*. New York: Cambridge University Press.

Brookings Institution Center on Urban and Metropolitan Policy. 2003. Philadelphia in focus: A profile from Census 2000. Living Cities: National Community Development Initiative.

Brown, Lyn Mikel. 2003. *Girlfighting: Betrayal and rejection among girls*. New York: New York University Press.

Chesney-Lind, Meda. 1997. *The female offender: Girls, women, and crime*. Thousand Oaks, Calif.: Sage Publications.

Chesney-Lind, Meda, and Michele Eliason. 2006. From invisible to incorrigible: The demonization of marginalized women and girls. *Crime, Media, Culture* 2 (1): 29–47.

Chesney-Lind, Meda, Merry Morash, and Katherine Irwin. 2007. Policing girlhood? Relational aggression and violence prevention. *Youth Violence and Juvenile Justice* 5 (3): 328–345.

Chesney-Lind, Meda, and Lisa Pasko. 2004. *The female offender: Girls, women, and crime.* Thousand Oaks, Calif.: Sage Publications.

Chesney-Lind, Meda, and Randall G. Shelden. 1992. *Girls, delinquency, and juvenile justice.* Pacific Grove, Calif.: Brooks/Cole Pub. Co.

Cole, Johnetta Betsch, and Beverly Guy-Sheftall. 2003. *Gender talk: The struggle for women's equality in African American communities.* New York: One World/Ballantine Books.

Collins, Patricia Hill. 2006. From black power to hip hop: Racism, nationalism, and feminism. Philadelphia: Temple University Press.

———. 2004. *Black sexual politics: African Americans, gender, and the new racism.* New York: Routledge.

———. [1990] 2000. *Black feminist thought: Knowledge, consciousness and the politics of empowerment.* New York: Routledge.

———. 1998. *Fighting words: Black women and the search for justice.* Minneapolis: University of Minnesota Press.

Connell, R. W., and James W. Messerschmidt. 2005. Hegemonic masculinity: Rethinking the concept. *Gender & Society* 19, no. 6 (December): 829–859.

Crenshaw, Kimberlé. 1995. Mapping the margins: Intersectionality, identity politics, and violence against women of color. In *Critical race theory: The key writings that formed the movement*, ed. Kimberlé Crenshaw, Neil Gotanda, Gary Peller, Kendall Thomas, 357–383. New York: New Press.

Daiute, Collette, and Michelle Fine. 2003. Youth perspectives on violence and injustice. *Journal of Social Issues* 59 (1): 1–14.

Dance, Lory J. 2002. *Tough fronts: The impact of street culture on schooling.* New York: Routledge Press.

DeKeseredy, Walter S., Martin D. Schwartz, Shahid Alvi, and Andreas Tomaszewski. 2003. Perceived collective eficacy and women's victimization in public housing. *Criminal Justice* 3 (1): 5–27.

Drake, St. Clair, and Horace R. Cayton. [1945] 1993. *Black metropolis: A study of Negro life in a Northern city.* Chicago: University of Chicago Press.

Du Bois, W.E.B. [1899] 1996. *The Philadelphia Negro: A social study.* Philadelphia: University of Pennsylvania Press.

Duneier, Mitchell. 1999. *Sidewalk.* New York: Farrar, Straus, and Giroux.

———. 1992. *Slim's table: Race, respectability, and masculinity.* Chicago: University of Chicago Press.

Dyson, Michael Eric. 2001. *Holler if you hear me: Searching for Tupac Shakur.* New York: Basic Books.

Elliot, Delbert S., S. Menard, B. Rankin, A. Elliott, W. J. Wilson, and D. Huizinga. 2006. Good kids from bad neighborhoods: Successful development in social context. New York: Cambridge University Press.

Emerson, R. M., R. I. Fretz, and L. L. Shaw. 1995. *Writing ethnographic fieldnotes.* Chicago: University of Chicago Press.

Erkut, S., J. P. Fields, R. Sing, and F. Marx. 1996. Diversity in girls' experiences: Feeling good about who you are. In Leadbeater and Way 1996.

Fenstermaker, Sarah, and Candace West, eds. 2002. *Doing gender, doing difference: Inequality, power, and institutional change.* New York: Routledge.

Ferguson, Ann A. 2000. *Bad boys: Public schools in the making of Black masculinity.* Ann Arbor: University of Michigan Press.

Fine, Michelle, Nick Freudenberg, Yasser Payne, Tiffany Perkins, Kersha Smith, and Katya Wanzer. 2003. "Anything can happen with police around": Urban youth evaluate strategies of surveillance in public places. *Journal of Social Issues* 59 (1): 141–158.

Fordham, Signithia, and John U. Ogbu. 1986. Black students' school success: Coping with the burden of acting white. *Urban Review* 18 (3): 176–206.

Freudenberg, N., L. Roberts, B. Richie, R. Taylor, K. McGillicuddy, and M. Greene. 1999. Coming up in the boogie down: The role of violence in the lives of adolescents in the South Bronx. *Health Education & Behavior* 26, no. 6 (December): 788–805.

George, Nelson. 1998. *Hip Hop America.* New York: Penguin.

Goffman, Erving. 1959. *The presentation of self in everyday life.* New York: Anchor Books.

Goodwin, Marjorie H. 1990. *He-said-she-said: Talk as social organization among Black children.* Bloomington: Indiana University Press.

Gutman, Herbert. 1976. *The Black family in slavery and freedom, 1750–1925.* New York: Random House.

Heimer, K., and S. De Coster. 1999. The gendering of violent delinquency. *Criminology* 37, no. 2.

Heimer, K., and C. Kruttschnitt. 2005. *Gender and crime: Patterns of victimization and offending.* New York: New York University Press.

Herring, Cedric, Verna M. Keith, and Hayward Derrick Horton, eds. 2004. *Skin deep: How race and complexion matter in the "color-blind" era.* Urbana: University of Illinois Press.

Higginbotham, Evelyn B. 1993. *Righteous discontent: The women's movement in the Black Baptist Church, 1880–1920.* Cambridge, Mass.: Harvard University Press.

Hughes, Everett C. 1945. Dilemmas and contradictions of status. *American Journal of Sociology* 50, no. 5 (March): 353.

Hughes, Everett C., and Helen MacGill Hughes. 1952. *Where peoples meet: Racial and ethnic frontiers.* Glencoe, Ill.: Free Press.

Hunter, Andrea. 1997. Counting on grandmothers: Black mothers' and fathers' reliance on grandmothers for parenting support. *Journal of Family Issues* 18 (3): 251–269.

Hunter, Margaret L. 2002. "If you're light you're alright": Light skin color as social capital for women of color. *Gender & Society* 16 (2): 175–193.

Irwin, Katherine. 2004. The violence of adolescent life: Experiencing and managing everyday threats. *Youth & Society* 35 (4): 452–479.

Jacobs, B. A., and J. Miller. 1998. Crack dealing, gender, and arrest avoidance. *Social Problems* 45, no. 4 (November).

Jones, Nikki. 2008. Working "the code": On girls, gender, and inner-city violence. *Australia and New Zealand Journal of Criminology* 41 (1): 63–83.

———. 2004a. "It's not where you live, it's how you live": How young women negotiate conflict and violence in the inner city. 2004. *Annals of the American Academy of Political and Social Science* 595 (September).

———. 2004b. A bad relationship: Violence in the lives of incarcerated Black women. *Souls: A Critical Journal of Black Politics, Culture and Society* 6, no. 1.

Katz, Jack. 1988. *Seductions of crime: Moral and sensual attractions in doing evil.* New York: Basic Books.

Keith, Verna M., and Cedric Herring. 1991. Skin tone and stratification in the Black community. *American Journal of Sociology* 97, no. 3 (November) 760–778.

Kingsley, G. T., and K.L.S. Pettit. 2003. *Concentrated poverty: A change in course.* Washington, D.C.: Urban Institute.

Kinney, Monica Yant, and Barbara Boyer. 2001. A long painful decline: West Philadelphia's Mill Creek has suffered neglect for years. Residents live in fear of the kind of violence that erupted last month. Editorial, *Philadelphia Inquirer,* January 7, D Edition, Sunday Review, D01.

Krivo, Lauren J., and Ruth D. Peterson. 1993. Racial segregation and Black urban homicide. *Social Forces* 71:5.

Kubrin, Charis E. 2005. Gangstas, thugs, and hustlas: Identity and the code of the street in rap music. *Social Problems* 52 (3): 360–378.

Kubrin, Charis E., and Ronald Weitzer. 2003. Retaliatory homicide: Concentrated disadvantage and neighborhood culture. *Social Problems* 50 (2): 157–180.

Ladner, Joyce. [1971] 1995. *Tomorrow's tomorrow: The Black woman.* Lincoln: University of Nebraska Press.

Lauritsen, J. L., and R. J. Sampson. 1998. Minorities, crime, and criminal justice. In *The handbook of crime and punishment,* ed. Michael Tonry. New York: Oxford University Press.

Leadbeater, J. R., and N. Way, eds. 1996. *Urban girls: Resisting stereotypes, creating identities.* New York: New York University Press.

Liebow, Elliot. 1967. *Tally's corner: A study of Negro streetcorner men.* Boston: Little, Brown.

Lorde, Audre. 1984. *Sister Outsider: Essays and Speeches*. Berkeley, Calif.: Crossing Press.

Maher, Lisa. 1997. *Sexed work: Gender, race and resistance in a Brooklyn drug market*. New York: Oxford University Press.

Massey, Douglass, and Nancy Denton. 1993. *American apartheid: Segregation and the making of the underclass*. Cambridge, Mass.: Harvard University Press.

Messerschmidt, James. 1993. *Masculinities and crime: Critique and reconceptualization of theory*. Lanham, Md.: Rowman & Littlefield.

Miller, Jody. 2008. *Getting played: African American girls, urban inequality, and gendered violence*. New York: New York University Press.

————. 2001. *One of the guys: Girls, gangs, and gender*. New York: Oxford University Press.

————. 1998. Up it up: Gender and the accomplishment of street robbery. *Criminology* 36, no. 1.

Mullins, C. W., R. T. Wright, and B. A. Jacobs. 2004. Gender, streetlife, and criminal retaliation. *Criminology* 42 (4): 911–940.

National Institute of Justice. 2004. When violence hits home: How economics and neighborhood play a role. Research Brief.

Ness, C. 2004. Why girls fight: Female youth violence in the inner city. *Annals of the American Academy of Political and Social Science* 595 (September).

New York Civil Liberties Union and American Civil Liberties Union. 2007. *Criminalizing the classroom: The over-policing of New York City schools*. Report written by Elora Mukherjee. New York.

Ogbu, John U. 2003. *Black American students in an affluent suburb: A study of academic disengagement*. Lawrence Earlbaum Associates.

Pastor, J., J. McCormick, and M. Fine. 1996. Makin' homes: An urban girl thing. In Leadbeater and Way 1996.

Pattillo, Mary. 2006. Critic, Author Meets Critic Session on *Promises I can keep: Why poor women put motherhood before marriage* by Kathryn Edin and Maria Kefalas (2005) at the American Sociological Association annual meeting, Montreal, Canada.

Peterson, Ruth D., and Lauren J. Krivo. 2005. Macrostructural analyses of race, ethnicity, and violent crime: Recent lessons and new directions for research. *Annual Review of Sociology* 31 (August): 331–356.

Peterson, Ruth D., Lauren J. Krivo, and John Hagan, eds. 2006. *The many colors of crime: Inequalities of race, ethnicity, and crime in America*. New York: New York University Press.

Peterson-Lewis, Sonja, and Lisa M. Bratton. 2004. Perceptions of acting Black among African American teens: Implications of racial dramaturgy for academic and social achievement. *Urban Review* 36, no. 2 (June): 81.

200   *References*

Philadelphia Police Department. 2006. Crime Statistics. http://www. ppdonline.org/hq_statistics.php (accessed March 30, 2006).

Putallaz, Martha, and Karen L. Bierman, eds. 2004. Aggression, antisocial behavior, and violence among girls: A developmental perspective. New York: Guilford Press.

Raphael, J. 2001. Public housing and domestic violence. *Violence Against Women* 7:699–706.

Renzetti, C. M., and S. L. Maier. 2002. "Private" crime in public housing: Violent victimization, fear of crime and social isolation among women public housing residents. *Women's Health and Urban Life* 1:46–65.

Richie, Beth. 1996. *Compelled to crime: The gender entrapment of battered Black women.* New York: Routledge.

Robert, Dorothy. 1998. *Killing the Black body: Race, reproduction, and the meaning of liberty.* New York: Pantheon Books.

Rose, Tricia. 1994. *Black noise: Rap music and Black culture in contemporary America.* Hanover, N.H.: Wesleyan University Press.

Roy, Kevin. 2004. Three-block fathers: Spatial perceptions and kinwork in low-income African American neighborhoods. *Social Problems* 51 (4): 528–548.

Sampson, Robert J., Stephen W. Raudenbush, and Felton Earls. 1997. Neighborhoods and violent crime: A multilevel study of collective efficacy. *Science* 277:918–924.

Sampson, R. J., and W. J. Wilson. 1995. Toward a theory of race, crime, and urban inequality. In *Crime and inequality,* ed. John Hagan and Ruth Peterson. Stanford, Calif.: Stanford University Press.

Segura, Denise. 1986. Chicanas and triple oppression in the labor force. In *Chicana voices: Intersections of class, race, and gender,* ed. T. Cordova. Austin, Tex.: Center for Mexican American Studies.

Sharpley-Whiting, T. Denean. 2007. *Pimps Up, Ho's Down: Hip Hop's Hold on Young Black Women.* New York: New York University Press.

Simmel, Georg. 1971. *On individuality and social forms.* Chicago: University of Chicago Press.

Simmons, Aishah. 2001. *NO! The Rape Documentary.*

Simmons, Rachel. 2002. *Odd girl out: The hidden culture of aggression in girls.* Orlando, Fla.: Harcourt.

Simpson, S. S. 1991. Caste, class, and violent crime: Explaining difference in female offending. *Criminology* 29, no. 1.

Smith, Linda Tuhiwai. 1999. *Decolonizing methodologies: Research and indigenous peoples.* New York: Zed Books.

Stack, Carol. 1974. *All our kin: Strategies for survival in a Black community.* New York: Basic Books.

Stewart, Eric A., Christopher J. Schreck, and Ronald L. Simons. 2006. "I ain't gonna let no one disrespect me": Does the code of the street reduce or increase violent victimization among African American adolescents? *Journal of Research in Crime and Delinquency* 43:337–351.

Stewart, Eric A., and Ronald L. Simons. 2009. *The code of the street and African American adolescent violence.* Washington, D.C.: U.S. Dept. of Justice, National Institute of Justice.

Thompson, Maxine, and Verna Keith. 2004. Copper brown and blue Black: Colorism and self evaluation. In Herring, Keith, and Horton 2004.

Twine, France Winddance. 2004. A white side of black Britain: The concept of racial literacy. *Ethnic and Racial Studies* 27, no. 6 (November): 878–907.

Twine, France Winddance, and Jonathan W. Warren. 2000. *Racing research, researching race: Methodological dilemmas in critical race studies.* New York: New York University Press.

U.S. Census Bureau. 2003. Poverty: 1999, Census 2000 Brief.

Wacquant, Loïc. 2002. *American Journal of Sociology* Review Symposium "Scrutinizing the Street: Poverty, Morality, and the Pitfalls of Urban Ethnography." *AJS* 107, no. 6 (May): 1468–1532.

Ward, Janie Victoria. 1996. Raising resisters: The role of truth telling in the psychological development of African American girls. In Leadbeater and Way 1996.

West, Candace, and Sarah Fenstermaker. 1995. Doing difference. *Gender & Society* 9:8–37.

West, Candace, and D. H. Zimmerman. 1987. Doing gender. *Gender & Society* 1:125–151.

Western, Bruce. 2006. *Punishment and equality in America.* New York: Russell Sage.

Whyte, William Foote. 1943. *Street corner society: The social structure of an Italian slum.* Chicago: University of Chicago Press.

Wilson, William Julius. 1996. *When work disappears: The world of the new urban poor.* New York: Vintage Books.

———. 1987. *The truly disadvantaged: The inner city, the underclass, and public policy.* Chicago: University of Chicago Press.

———. 1980. *The declining significance of race: Blacks and changing American institutions.* Chicago: University of Chicago Press.

Winant, Howard. 2006. Race and racism: Toward a global future. *Ethnic and Racial Studies* 29, no. 5 (September).

Wiseman, Rosalind. 2003. *Queen bees and wannabes: Helping your daughter survive cliques, gossip, boyfriends, and other realities of adolescence.* New York: Three Rivers Press.

Zernike, Kate. 2006. Violent crime rising sharply in some cities. *New York Times*, National, February 12.

Zucchino, David, and Monica Yant Kinney. 2001. Life led 10 people into a crack house; 7 never made it out. It was the city's worst mass murder. They got "caught in the madness." *Philadelphia Inquirer*, July 22, Sunday City-D Edition, Local, A01.

Index

abortion, 122, 123, 129–130, 136, 143–144, 146
accountability: and "code of the street," 5, 7, 153; and gender, 7–8
All Our Kin (Stack), 189n7
American Apartheid (Massey and Denton), 183n4
American Civil Liberties Union, 183n2
analytic induction method, 186n20
Anderson, Elijah, 118, 126; campaigns for respect, 12; "code of the street," 5; code-switching, 11, 155, 165; decency, 9–10, 50; "the dream" and "the game," 118, 126; and Du Bois, 176; ethnographies, 165, 178; "go for bad," 78; inner-city grandmothers, 33, 192n2; manhood and the code of the street, 5–6, 184nn8,9; observant participant, 16, 167; perceptions of police, 4; relationship between neighborhood circumstances and the use of violence, 184; social organization of the

corner, 23, 24; staging areas, 54; "street" and "decent" orientations, 9–10; structural changes in the inner city, 3; urban ethnography, 194n3; urban sociology, 180
anger: and aggression and violence, 82; of girl fighters, 84; Lorde on, 190n8
arrest, mandatory, for domestic violence, 118
associates: versus friends, 54–55; and loyalty links, 55
authenticity tests, for field research, 169–173

baby's father relationship: expectations of mothers, 118, 126; having a baby *with* someone, 126–130, 143–146; and making a family, 61
Banks, Ingrid, 48, 188n2
Becker, Howard, 165, 186n20
behavior modification, 168
Bettie, Julie, 188n6
Bierman, Karen L., 189n8
birth control: Depo-Provera and Black women, 191n11; and negotiations with sexual partners, 137–138

About the Author

NIKKI JONES is an assistant professor in the Department of Sociology at the University of California, Santa Barbara. She is a William T. Grant Foundation Scholar (2007–12).